denise levertov
selected poems

Books by Denise Levertov

Poetry
The Double Image
Here and Now
Overland to the Islands
With Eyes at the Back of Our Heads
The Jacob's Ladder
O Taste and See
The Sorrow Dance
Relearning the Alphabet
To Stay Alive
Footprints
The Freeing of the Dust
Life in the Forest
Collected Earlier Poems 1940–1960
Candles in Babylon
Poems 1960–1967
Oblique Prayers
Poems 1968–1972
Breathing the Water
A Door in the Hive
Evening Train
Sands of the Well
The Life Around Us
The Stream and the Sapphire
This Great Unknowing: Last Poems
Poems 1972–1982

Prose
New & Selected Essays
Tesserae: Memories & Suppositions
The Letters of Denise Levertov & William Carlos Williams

Translations
Guillevic/Selected Poems
Joubert/Black Iris (Copper Canyon Press)

denise levertov
selected poems

with a preface
by robert creeley

edited and with an afterword
by paul a. lacey

a new directions book

Manufactured in the United States of America
First published clothbound in 2002 and in paper as NDP968 in 2003

LIBRARY OF CONGRESS CATALOGING-IN-PUBLICATION DATA
Levertov, Denise, 1923–1997
[Poems. Selections]
The selected poems of Denise Levertov / with a preface by Robert
Creeley ; edited and with an afterword by Paul A. Lacey.
p. cm.
Includes index.
ISBN 978-0-8112-1554-1 (alk. paper)
I. Lacey, Paul A. II. Title.
PS3562.E8876 A6 2002
811'.54—dc21   2002011891

10 9 8 7 6 5

New Directions Books are published for James Laughlin
by New Directions Publishing Corporation
80 Eighth Avenue, New York 10011

Contents

Now and again it must be that someone's death leaves such an emptiness among their company that the loss feels irreparable. So one might well write of Denise Levertov what she then said of her own elders in her poem "September 1961"— "This is the year the old ones,/the old great ones/leave us alone on the road.//The road leads to the sea./We have the words in our pockets, obscure directions…"

> But for us the road
> unfurls itself, we count the
> words in our pockets, we wonder
>
> how it will be without them, we don't
> stop walking, we know
> there is far to go, sometimes
>
> we think the night wind carries
> a smell of the sea…

Poets are a company and poetry must finally be a tribal art despite the fierceness of contest, which sometimes preoccupies its persons. As always they come from all manner of situation, rich and poor, near and far. It is especially dear, however, that Denise Levertov should have been born in Ilford, a suburb of London, in 1923, the youngest daughter of a Welsh mother, Beatrice Adelaide Spooner-Jones, and a Russian immigrant Jewish scholar converted to Anglicanism, Paul Philip Levertoff. Even more interesting is the fact that she never had formal education but was tutored at home by her parents, while otherwise an active apprentice dancer at Sadler's Wells. Her adolescence ends in the bleak chaos of the Second World War with its devastating bombings of London, during which time she serves as a civilian nurse in various hospitals.

Just after the war's end she met her husband-to-be, the American writer Mitchell Goodman, at a youth hostel in Switzerland. This chance encounter changed everything, bringing her thereby to live in this country and so to become the singular and profoundly defining poet of our own time and place. There is neither reason nor need to rehearse now the details of her many books or of the years spent as a decisive teacher at universities such as Tufts, Brandeis, or Stanford—nor even to review her unremitting political activities, so committed to confronting the despairs of our common world. Better now to remember the intensely human presence, the vivid rapport she has with the aging Williams, the impression she first makes on Kenneth Rexroth, causing him to call her "Dante's Beatrice incarnate," the way she manages to acclimate and then to find her necessary world. Who can ever forget her, who saw her just then—the extraordinary, utterly *beautiful* energy, the compact, *physical* strength of movement—all of which became manifest of her art?

Her husband, Mitch, was my old classmate and so I knew Denise in those moving, early days. Their young family visited our makeshift home in New Hampshire and later I became in turn their frequent, almost awkward "guest" in New York. But most significant was the year we spent as neighbors in the south of France, where she and I would spend hours sitting at the edge of their orchard in Puyricard. We talked as only the young can—of our master Williams' line, of how to locate stress, how to *measure,* to keep the physical fact of sound and rhythm explicit. I recall one time we were all to cycle into Aix for a performance of Mozart, down the steep route alongside Mt. Sainte-Victoire, where Cézanne once had his studio. The road went through the wheat fields of various farmers, whose fierce, bad-tempered dogs came snarling after us as we pedaled past, racing for our lives. The evening, however, it was the sudden failure of Denise's brakes, which almost proved disastrous. One moment she was beside us, the next she was gathering speed and outdistancing us as her bike hurtled forward and then out of sight, around a bend. We tried to keep up but she was gone—and so we made our way down, fearful of the apparent outcome. But once there, she suddenly reappeared, having shot all through the city's early evening traffic to the far side where an incline let her finally come to a stop. Amazingly I think that was that, and we went on to the concert without further comment.

If one wanted to say what it was seemed most insistent in either her work or her person, it would be—always for me—the fact of *body*, the immediacy of that presence in all she wrote or was. Her friends will forever remember the wild gutsy chuckling, the giggling bursts of delight, that were such pleasure to witness. She moved always to the physical term, call it—and probably she herself puts it most simply in a characteristic line: "If we're going to be here, let's be here now…" She was, always.

The exceptional grace—a dancer's, I liked to think—of her work, the movement so particular to a complex of thought and feeling, accomplished a rare unity. That quality is present in all she does, whether in the early poems of marriage, friends and family, or else those later of an increasing outrage and despair as the general world in which she lives sinks more deeply into war and righteous judgment. There is no one who writes more particularly of what being a woman constitutes. "Hypocrite Women," "Losing Track," "The Ache of Marriage," "Stepping Westward"—so many. Here it was that her powers first gathered and declared themselves, unequivocally forthright and particular.

Her old and constant friend Robert Duncan, despite their late questions of one another, best defines the character of "responsibility" which was Denise's: "Responsibility is the ability to respond." Hers was impeccable—in all respects, in all reference. She had a way of seeing the world that was perhaps without a usual shading. But what use the endless accommodation, the temporizing, the irresolution? She would have none of it, even less as she grew older. People could not be brutalized and murdered while we waited, still patient, to understand.

In the very last years she became a Catholic, and I wondered about that for my own reasons, curious that she should, as a woman, accept the situation of that belief. Very probably I missed the point entirely—and presumed that her choice was among possibilities, whereas I now see it was to come into a company, a gathering of all, a determined yielding of such distinction and isolating privilege, which may well have persuaded her. I miss her very much—as I am sure all must who knew her in whatever way—who read her extraordinary poems or heard her read them with such melodious clarity and precision. I depended upon her integrity, that she was dogged, determined, flooded with purpose. Because a moment later her wit was like a sudden ripple, a streak of sunlight, the chitter of some hidden bird. One was so thankful that she was there. Her heart was so much herself, so literal. She was a great and abiding poet, a wonderfully explicit human. One will not forget how much she cared for *life,* our lives, as people, the world forever the one in which we all must finally learn to live while we can.

ROBERT CREELEY

*(Originally an address to
the American Academy of Arts and Letters,
in 1998, in honor of the life and work
of Denise Levertov)*

denise levertov
selected poems

Listening to Distant Guns

The roses tremble; oh, the sunflower's eye
Is opened wide in sad expectancy.
Westward and back the circling swallows fly,
The rook's battalions dwindle near the hill.

That low pulsation in the east is war:
No bell now breaks the evening's silent dream.
The bloodless clarity of evening's sky
Betrays no whisper of the battle-scream.

Childhood's End

The world alive with love, where leaves tremble,
systole and diastole marking miraculous hours,
is burning round the children where they lie
deep in caressing grasses all the day,
and feverish words of once upon a time
assail their hearts with languor and with swans.
The pebble's shadow quivers in the sun;
the light grows low, and they become
tuned to the love and death of day, the instruments
of life and dream, as Syrinx flying
in fear from unimaginable sound, became
music's green channel; then they rise and go
up the inevitable stony slope
to search untravelled valleys for the land
of wonder and of loss; but on that hill
they find it, wound about them like a cloud.

Some are too much at home in the role of wanderer,
watcher, listener; who, by lamplit doors
that open only to another's knock,
commune with shadows and are happier
with ghosts than living guests in a warm house.
They drift about the darkening city squares,
coats blown in evening winds and fingers feeling
familiar holes in pockets, thinking: Life
has always been a counterfeit, a dream
where dreaming figures danced behind the glass.
Yet as they work, or absently stand at a window
letting a tap run and the plates lie wet,
while the bright rain softly shines upon slates,
they feel the whole of life is theirs, the music,
"colour, and warmth, and light"; hands held
safe in the hands of love; and trees beside them
dark and gentle, growing as they grow,
a part of the world with fire and house and child.
The undertone of all their solitude
is the unceasing question, "Who am I?
A shadow's image on the rainy pavement,
walking in wonder past the vivid windows,
a half-contented guest among my ghosts?
Or one who, imagining light, air, sun,
can now take root in life, inherit love?"

London, 1946

Too easy: to write of miracles, dreams where the famous give
mysterious utterance to silent truth;
to confuse snow with the stars,
simulate a star's fantastic wisdom.

Easy like the willow to lament,
rant in trampled roads where pools
are red with sorrowful fires, and sullen rain
drips from the willows' ornamental leaves;
or die in words and angrily turn
to pace like ghosts about the walls of war.

But difficult when, innocent and cold,
day, a bird over a hill, flies in
—resolving anguish to a strange perspective,
a scene within a marble; returning
the brilliant shower of coloured dreams to dust,
a smell of fireworks lingering by canals
on autumn evenings—difficult to write
of the real image, real hand, the heart
of day or autumn beating steadily:
to speak of human gestures, clarify
all the context of a simple phrase
—the hour, the shadow, the fire,
the loaf on a bare table.

Hard, under the honest sun, to weigh
a word until it balances with love—
burden of happiness on fearful shoulders;
in the ease of daylight to discover
what measure has its music, and achieve
the unhaunted country of the final poem.

Sicily, 1948

The earthwoman by her oven
        tends her cakes of good grain.
The waterwoman's children
are spindle thin.
                The earthwoman
        has oaktree arms. Her children
full of blood and milk
        stamp through the woods shouting.
        The waterwoman
        sings gay songs in a sad voice
                with her moonshine children.
When the earthwoman
has had her fill of the good day
        she curls to sleep in her warm hut
        a dark fruitcake sleep
but the waterwoman
                goes dancing in the misty lit-up town
        in dragonfly dresses and blue shoes.

The Marriage

You have my
attention: which is
a tenderness, beyond
what I may say. And I have
your constancy to
                something beyond myself.
The force
of your commitment charges us—we live
in the sweep of it, taking courage
one from the other.

The Marriage (II)

I want to speak to you.
To whom else should I speak?
It is you who make
a world to speak of.
In your warmth the
fruits ripen—all the
apples and pears that grow
on the south wall of my
head. If you listen
it rains for them, then
they drink. If you
speak in response
the seeds
jump into the ground.
Speak or be silent: your silence
will speak to me.

Laying the Dust

What a sweet smell rises
  when you lay the dust—
bucket after bucket of water thrown
on the yellow grass.
     The water
flashes
each time you
make it leap—
  arching its glittering back.
The sound of
    more water
pouring into the pail
almost quenches my thirst.
Surely when flowers
grow here, they'll not
smell sweeter than this
    wet ground, suddenly black.

5

From the tawny light
from the rainy nights
from the imagination finding
itself and more than itself
alone and more than alone
at the bottom of the well where the moon lives,
can you pull me

into December? a lowland
of space, perception of space
towering of shadows of clouds blown upon
clouds over
                new ground, new made
under heavy December footsteps? *the only
way to live?*

The flawed moon
acts on the truth, and makes
an autumn of tentative
silences.
You lived, but somewhere else,
your presence touched others, ring upon ring,
and changed. Did you think
I would not change?

                The black moon
turns away, its work done. A tenderness,
unspoken autumn.
We are faithful
only to the imagination. *What the
imagination
                seizes
as beauty must be truth.* What holds you
to what you see of me is
that grasp alone.

6

Overland to the Islands

Let's go—much as that dog goes,
intently haphazard. The
Mexican light on a day that
'smells like autumn in Connecticut'
makes iris ripples on his
black gleaming fur—and that too
is as one would desire—a radiance
consorting with the dance.
                    Under his feet
rocks and mud, his imagination, sniffing,
engaged in its perceptions—dancing
edgeways, there's nothing
the dog disdains on his way,
nevertheless he
keeps moving, changing
pace and approach but
not direction—'every step an arrival.'

The Instant

'We'll go out before breakfast, and get
some mushrooms,' says my mother.

Early, early: the sun
risen, but hidden in mist

the square house left behind
sleeping, filled with sleepers;

up the dewy hill, quietly, with baskets.

Mushrooms firm, cold;
        tussocks of dark grass, gleam of webs,
turf soft and cropped. Quiet and early. And no valley,

no hills: clouds about our knees, tendrils
of cloud in our hair. Wet scrags
of wool caught in barbed wire, gorse
looming, without scent.
                         Then ah! suddenly
the lifting of it, the mist rolls
      quickly away, and far, far—

      'Look!' she grips me, 'It is
                   Eryri!
                   It's Snowdon, fifty
      miles away!'—the voice
a wave rising to Eryri,
falling.
         Snowdon, home
of eagles, resting place of
Merlin, core of Wales.

                   Light
graces the mountainhead
for a lifetime's look, before the mist
      draws in again.

                                   Illustrious Ancestors

The Rav
of Northern White Russia declined,
in his youth, to learn the
language of birds, because
the extraneous did not interest him; nevertheless
when he grew old it was found
he understood them anyway, having
listened well, and as it is said, 'prayed
                   with the bench and the floor.' He used
what was at hand—as did

Angel Jones of Mold, whose meditations
were sewn into coats and britches.
                    Well, I would like to make,
thinking some line still taut between me and them,
poems direct as what the birds said,
hard as a floor, sound as a bench,
mysterious as the silence when the tailor
would pause with his needle in the air.

Action

I can lay down that history
I can lay down my glasses
I can lay down the imaginary lists
of what to forget and what must be
done. I can shake the sun
out of my eyes and lay everything down
on the hot sand, and cross
the whispering threshold and walk
right into the clear sea, and float there,
my long hair floating, and fishes
vanishing all around me. Deep water.
Little by little one comes to know
the limits and depths of power.

Merritt Parkway

As if it were
forever that they move, that we
keep moving—

Under a wan sky where
as the lights went on a star
pierced the haze & now
follows steadily
a constant
above our six lanes
the dreamlike continuum . . .

And the people—ourselves!
the humans from inside the
cars, apparent
only at gasoline stops
unsure,
eyeing each other

drink coffee hastily at the
slot machines & hurry
back to the cars
vanish
into them forever, to
keep moving—

Houses now & then beyond the
sealed road, the trees / trees, bushes
passing by, passing
        the cars that
                keep moving ahead of
        us, past us, pressing behind us
                                and
                        over left, those that come
                toward us shining too brightly
moving relentlessly

        in six lanes, gliding
        north & south, speeding with
        a slurred sound—

With eyes at the back of our heads
we see a mountain
not obstructed with woods but laced
here and there with feathery groves.

The doors before us in a façade
that perhaps has no house in back of it
are too narrow, and one is set high
with no doorsill. The architect sees

the imperfect proposition and
turns eagerly to the knitter.
Set it to rights!
The knitter begins to knit.

For we want
to enter the house, if there is a house,
to pass through the doors at least
into whatever lies beyond them,

we want to enter the arms
of the knitted garment. As one
is re-formed, so the other,
in proportion.

When the doors widen
when the sleeves admit us
the way to the mountain will clear,
the mountain we see with
eyes at the back of our heads, mountain
green, mountain
cut of limestone, echoing
with hidden rivers, mountain
of short grass and subtle shadows.

I like to find
what's not found
at once, but lies

within something of another nature,
in repose, distinct.
Gull feathers of glass, hidden

in white pulp: the bones of squid
which I pull out and lay
blade by blade on the draining board—

     tapered as if for swiftness, to pierce
     the heart, but fragile, substance
     belying design.   Or a fruit, *mamey,*

cased in rough brown peel, the flesh
rose-amber, and the seed:
the seed a stone of wood, carved and

polished, walnut-colored, formed
like a brazilnut, but large,
large enough to fill
the hungry palm of a hand.

I like the juicy stem of grass that grows
within the coarser leaf folded round,
and the butteryellow glow
in the narrow flute from which the morning-glory
opens blue and cool on a hot morning.

Green Snake, when I hung you round my neck
and stroked your cold, pulsing throat
       as you hissed to me, glinting
arrowy gold scales, and I felt
       the weight of you on my shoulders,
and the whispering silver of your dryness
       sounded close at my ears—

Green Snake—I swore to my companions that certainly
       you were harmless! But truly
I had no certainty, and no hope, only desiring
       to hold you, for that joy,
               which left
a long wake of pleasure, as the leaves moved
and you faded into the pattern
of grass and shadows, and I returned
smiling and haunted, to a dark morning.

Obsessions

Maybe it is true we have to return
to the black air of ashcan city
because it is there the most life was burned,

as ghosts or criminals return?
But no, the city has no monopoly
of intense life. The dust burned

golden or violet in the wide land
to which we ran away, images
of passion sprang out of the land

14

as whirlwinds or red flowers, your hands
opened in anguish or clenched in violence
under that sun, and clasped my hands

in that place to which we will not return
where so much happened that no one else noticed,
where the city's ashes that we brought with us
flew into the intense sky still burning.

The Dead

Earnestly I looked
into their abandoned faces
at the moment of death and while
I bandaged their slack jaws and
straightened waxy unresistant limbs and plugged
the orifices with cotton
but like everyone else I learned
each time nothing new, only that
as it were, a music, however harsh, that held us
however loosely, had stopped, and left
a heavy thick silence in its place.

Terror

Face-down; odor
of dusty carpet. The grip
of anguished stillness.

Then your naked voice, your
head knocking the wall, sideways,
the beating of trapped thoughts against iron.

If I remember, how is it
my face shows
barely a line? Am I
a monster, to sing
in the wind on this sunny hill

and not taste the dust always,
and not hear
that rending, that retching?
How did morning come, and the days
that followed, and quiet nights?

A Common Ground

i

To stand on common ground
here and there gritty with pebbles
yet elsewhere 'fine and mellow—
uncommon fine for ploughing'

there to labor
planting the vegetable words
diversely in their order
that they come to virtue!

To reach those shining pebbles,
that soil where uncommon men
have labored in their virtue
and left a store

of seeds for planting!
To crunch on words
grown in grit or fine
crumbling earth, sweet

to eat and sweet
to be given, to be eaten
in common, by laborer
and hungry wanderer . . .

ii

In time of blossoming,
of red
buds, of red
margins upon
white petals among the
new green, of coppery
leaf-buds still weakly
folded, fuzzed
with silver hairs—

when on the grass verges
or elephant-hide rocks, the lunch hour
expands, the girls
laugh at the sun, men
in business suits awkwardly
recline, the petals
float and fall into
crumpled wax-paper, cartons
of hot coffee—

to speak as the sun's
deep tone of May gold speaks
or the spring chill in the rock's shadow,
a piercing minor scale running across the flesh
aslant—or petals
that dream their way
(speaking by being white
by being
curved, green-centered, falling
already while their tree
is half-red with buds) into

human lives! Poems stirred
into paper coffee-cups, eaten
with petals on rye in the
sun—the cold shadows in back,
and the traffic grinding the
borders of spring—entering
human lives forever,
unobserved, a spring element . . .

iii

> . . . everything in the world must
> excel itself to be itself.
>
> *Pasternak*

Not 'common speech'
a dead level
but the uncommon speech of paradise,
tongue in which oracles
speak to beggars and pilgrims:

not illusion but what Whitman called
'the path
between reality and the soul,'
a language
excelling itself to be itself,

speech akin to the light
with which at day's end and day's
renewal, mountains
sing to each other across the cold valleys.

Come into Animal Presence

Come into animal presence.
No man is so guileless as
the serpent. The lonely white
rabbit on the roof is a star
twitching its ears at the rain.
The llama intricately
folding its hind legs to be seated
not disdains but mildly
disregards human approval.
What joy when the insouciant
armadillo glances at us and doesn't
quicken his trotting
across the track into the palm brush.

What is this joy? That no animal
falters, but knows what it must do?
That the snake has no blemish,
that the rabbit inspects his strange surroundings
in white star-silence? The llama
rests in dignity, the armadillo
has some intention to pursue in the palm-forest.
Those who were sacred have remained so,
holiness does not dissolve, it is a presence
of bronze, only the sight that saw it
faltered and turned from it.
An old joy returns in holy presence.

A Map of the Western Part of the
County of Essex in England

Something forgotten for twenty years: though my fathers
and mothers came from Cordova and Vitepsk and Caernarvon,
and though I am a citizen of the United States and less a
stranger here than anywhere else, perhaps,
I am Essex-born:
Cranbrook Wash called me into its dark tunnel,
the little streams of Valentines heard my resolves,
Roding held my head above water when I thought it was
drowning me; in Hainault only a haze of thin trees
stood between the red doubledecker buses and the boar-hunt,
the spirit of merciful Phillipa glimmered there.
Pergo Park knew me, and Clavering, and Havering-atte-
      Bower,
Stanford Rivers lost me in osier beds, Stapleford Abbots
sent me safe home on the dark road after Simeon-quiet
      evensong,
Wanstead drew me over and over into its basic poetry,
in its serpentine lake I saw bass-viols among the golden dead
      leaves,
through its trees the ghost of a great house. In
Ilford High Road I saw the multitudes passing pale under the
light of flaring sundown, seven kings
in somber starry robes gathered at Seven Kings
the place of law
where my birth and marriage are recorded
and the death of my father. Woodford Wells
where an old house was called The Naked Beauty (a white
statue forlorn in its garden)
saw the meeting and parting of two sisters,
(forgotten? and further away
the hill before Thaxted? where peace befell us? not once
but many times?).
All the Ivans dreaming of their villages
all the Marias dreaming of their walled cities,

picking up fragments of New World slowly,
not knowing how to put them together nor how to join
image with image, now I know how it was with you, an old
    map
made long before I was born shows ancient
rights of way where I walked when I was ten burning with
    desire
for the world's great splendors, a child who traced voyages
indelibly all over the atlas, who now in a far country
remembers the first river, the first
field, bricks and lumber dumped in it ready for building,
that new smell, and remembers
the walls of the garden, the first light.

Three Meditations

i

the only object is
a man, carved
out of himself, so wrought he
fills his given space, makes
traceries sufficient to
others' needs
                        (here is
social action, for the poet,
anyway, his
politics, his
news)

Charles Olson

Breathe deep of the
freshly gray morning air, mild
spring of the day.
Let the night's dream-planting
bear leaves
and light up the death-mirrors with
shining petals.
Stand fast in thy place:
remember, Caedmon
turning from song was met
in his cow-barn by One who set him
to sing the beginning.
Live
in thy fingertips and in thy
hair's rising; hunger
be thine, food
be thine and what wine
will not shrivel thee.
Breathe deep of
evening, be with the
rivers of tumult, sharpen
thy wits to know power and be
humble.

22

ii

Barbarians
throng the straight roads of
my empire, converging
on black Rome.
There is darkness in me.
Silver sunrays
sternly, in tenuous joy
cut through its folds:
mountains
arise from cloud.
Who was it yelled, cracking
the glass of delight?
Who sent the child
sobbing to bed, and woke it
later to comfort it?
I, I, I, I.
I multitude, I tyrant,
I angel, I you, you
world, battlefield, stirring
with unheard litanies, sounds of piercing
green half-smothered by
strewn bones.

iii

Death in the grassblade
a dull
substance, heading blindly
for the bone

and bread preserved without
virtue,
sweet grapes sour to the children's children.

We breathe an ill wind,
nevertheless our kind
in mushroom multitudes
jostles for elbow-room
moonwards

an equalization of
hazards
bringing the poet
back to song
as before

to sing of death
as before
and life, while he
has it, energy

being in him a singing,
a beating of gongs, efficacious
to drive away devils,
response to

the wonder that
as before
shows a double face,

to be
what he is
being his virtue

filling his whole space
so no devil
may enter.

The stairway is not
a thing of gleaming strands
a radiant evanescence
for angels' feet that only glance in their tread, and need not
touch the stone.

It is of stone.
A rosy stone that takes
a glowing tone of softness
only because behind it the sky is a doubtful, a doubting
night gray.

A stairway of sharp
angles, solidly built.
One sees that the angels must spring
down from one step to the next, giving a little
lift of the wings:

and a man climbing
must scrape his knees, and bring
the grip of his hands into play. The cut stone
consoles his groping feet. Wings brush past him.
The poem ascends.

The Tulips

Red tulips
living into their death
flushed with a wild blue

tulips
becoming wings
ears of the wind
jackrabbits rolling their eyes

west wind
shaking the loose pane

some petals fall
with that sound one
listens for

During the Eichmann Trial

i   When We Look Up

> When we look up
> each from his being
> *Robert Duncan*

He had not looked,
pitiful man whom none

pity, whom all
must pity if they look

into their own face (given
only by glass, steel, water

barely known) all
who look up

to see—how many
faces?   How many

seen in a lifetime? (Not those
that flash by, but those

into which the gaze wanders
and is lost

and returns to tell
Here is a mystery,

**a person, an
other, an I?**

Count them.
Who are five million?)

'I was used from the nursery
to obedience

all my life . . .
Corpselike

obedience.' Yellow
calmed him later—

'a charming picture'
yellow of autumn leaves in

Wienerwald, a little
railroad station
nineteen-o-eight, Lemburg,

yellow sun
on the stepmother's teatable

Franz Joseph's beard
blessing his little ones.

It was the yellow
of the stars too,

stars that marked
those in whose faces

you had not
looked. 'They were cast out

as if they were
some animals, some beasts.'

'And what would disobedience
have brought me? And

whom would it have served?'
'I did not let my thoughts

dwell on this—I had
seen it and that was

enough.' (The words
'slur into a harsh babble')

'A spring of blood
gushed from the earth.'
Miracle

unsung. I see
a spring of blood gush from the earth—

Earth cannot swallow
so much at once

a fountain
rushes towards the sky

unrecognized
a sign—.

Pity this man who saw it
whose obedience continued—

he, you, I, which shall I say?
He stands

isolate in a bulletproof
witness-stand of glass,

a cage, where we may view
ourselves, an apparition

telling us something he
does not know: we are members

one of another.

The ache of marriage:

thigh and tongue, beloved,
are heavy with it,
it throbs in the teeth

We look for communion
and are turned away, beloved,
each and each

It is leviathan and we
in its belly
looking for joy, some joy
not to be known outside it

two by two in the ark of
the ache of it.

Song for Ishtar

The moon is a sow
and grunts in my throat
Her great shining shines through me
so the mud of my hollow gleams
and breaks in silver bubbles

She is a sow
and I a pig and a poet

When she opens her white
lips to devour me I bite back
and laughter rocks the moon

In the black of desire
we rock and grunt, grunt and
shine

Claritas

i

The All-Day Bird, the artist,
whitethroated sparrow,
striving
in hope and
good faith to make his notes
ever more precise, closer
to what he knows.

ii

There is the proposition
and the development.
The way
one grows from the other.
The All-Day Bird
ponders.

iii

May the first note
be round enough
and those that follow

31

fine, fine as
sweetgrass,
            prays
the All-Day Bird.

iv

Fine
as the tail of a lizard,
as a leaf of
chives—
the *shadow of a difference*
falling between
note and note,
a *hair's breadth*
defining them.

v

The dew is on the vineleaves.
My tree
is lit with the
break of day.

vi

Sun
light.
      Light
light light light.

Two girls discover
the secret of life
in a sudden line of
poetry.

I who don't know the
secret wrote
the line. They
told me

(through a third person)
they had found it
but not what it was
not even

what line it was. No doubt
by now, more than a week
later, they have forgotten
the secret,

the line, the name of
the poem. I love them
for finding what
I can't find,

and for loving me
for the line I wrote,
and for forgetting it
so that

a thousand times, till death
finds them, they may
discover it again, in other
lines

in other
happenings. And for
wanting to know it,
for

assuming there is
such a secret, yes,
for that
most of all.

September 1961

This is the year the old ones,
the old great ones
leave us alone on the road.

The road leads to the sea.
We have the words in our pockets,
obscure directions. The old ones

have taken away the light of their presence,
we see it moving away over a hill
off to one side.

They are not dying,
they are withdrawn
into a painful privacy

learning to live without words.
E.P. "It looks like dying"—Williams: "I can't
describe to you what has been

happening to me"—
H.D. "unable to speak."
The darkness

twists itself in the wind, the stars
are small, the horizon
ringed with confused urban light-haze.

They have told us
the road leads to the sea,
and given

the language into our hands.
We hear
our footsteps each time a truck

has dazzled past us and gone
leaving us new silence.
One can't reach

the sea on this endless
road to the sea unless
one turns aside at the end, it seems,

follows
the owl that silently glides above it
aslant, back and forth,

and away into deep woods.

But for us the road
unfurls itself, we count the
words in our pockets, we wonder

how it will be without them, we don't
stop walking, we know
there is far to go, sometimes

we think the night wind carries
a smell of the sea. . .

The world is
not with us enough.
O taste and see

the subway Bible poster said,
meaning **The Lord,** meaning
if anything all that lives
to the imagination's tongue,

grief, mercy, language,
tangerine, weather, to
breathe them, bite,
savor, chew, swallow, transform

into our flesh our
deaths, crossing the street, plum, quince,
living in the orchard and being

hungry, and plucking
the fruit.

The river in its abundance
many-voiced
all about us as we stood
on a warm rock to wash

slowly
smoothing in long
                    sliding strokes
our soapy hands along each other's
slippery cool bodies

quiet and slow in the midst of
the quick of the
sounding river

our hands were
flames
stealing upon quickened flesh until

no part of us but was
sleek and
on fire

Hand of man
hewed from
the mottled rock

almost touching
as Adam the hand of God

smallest inviolate
stone violet

The Disclosure

From the shrivelling gray
silk of its cocoon
a creature slowly
        is pushing out
to stand clear—
                not a butterfly,
                    petal that floats at will across
                    the summer breeze

                not a furred
                moth of the night
                    crusted with indecipherable
                    gold—

some primal-shaped, plain-winged, day-flying thing.

About Marriage

Don't lock me in wedlock, I want
marriage, an
encounter—

I told you about the
green light of
May

      (a veil of quiet befallen
      the downtown park,
      late

      Saturday after
      noon, long
      shadows and cool

      air, scent of
      new grass,
      fresh leaves,

      blossom on the threshold of
      abundance—

      and the birds I met there,
      birds of passage breaking their journey,
      three birds each of a different species:

      the azalea-breasted with round poll, dark,
      the brindled, merry, mousegliding one,
      and the smallest, golden as gorse and wearing
      a black Venetian mask

      and with them the three douce hen-birds
      feathered in tender, lively brown—

I stood
a half-hour under the enchantment,
no-one passed near,
the birds saw me and

let me be
near them.)

It's not
irrelevant:
I would be
met

and meet you
so,
in a green

airy space, not
locked in.

The Prayer

At Delphi I prayed
to Apollo
that he maintain in me
the flame of the poem

and I drank of the brackish
spring there, dazed by the
gong beat of the sun,
mistaking it,

as I shrank from the eagle's
black shadow crossing
that sky of cruel blue,
for the Pierian Spring—

and soon after
vomited my moussaka
and then my guts writhed
for some hours with diarrhea

until at dusk
among the stones of the goatpaths
breathing dust
I questioned my faith, or

within it wondered
if the god mocked me.
But since then, though it flickers or
shrinks to a

blue bead on the wick,
there's that in me that
burns and chills, blackening
my heart with its soot,

flaring in laughter, stinging
my feet into a dance, so that
I think sometimes not Apollo heard me
but a different god.

Hypocrite women, how seldom we speak
of our own doubts, while dubiously
we mother man in his doubt!

And if at Mill Valley perched in the trees
the sweet rain drifting through western air
a white sweating bull of a poet told us

our cunts are ugly—why didn't we
admit we have thought so too? (And
what shame? They are not for the eye!)

No, they are dark and wrinkled and hairy,
caves of the Moon . . .   And when a
dark humming fills us, a

coldness towards life,
we are too much women to
own to such unwomanliness.

Whorishly with the psychopomp
we play and plead—and say
nothing of this later.   And our dreams,

with what frivolity we have pared them
like toenails, clipped them like ends of
split hair.

There's in my mind a woman
of innocence, unadorned but

fair-featured, and smelling of
apples or grass. She wears

a utopian smock or shift, her hair
is light brown and smooth, and she

is kind and very clean without
ostentation—
           but she has
no imagination.
              And there's a
turbulent moon-ridden girl

or old woman, or both,
dressed in opals and rags, feathers

and torn taffeta,
who knows strange songs—

but she is not kind.

Something hangs in back of me,
I can't see it, can't move it.

I know it's black,
a hump on my back.

It's heavy. You
can't see it.

What's in it? Don't tell me
you don't know. It's

what you told me about—
black

inimical power, cold
whirling out of it and

around me and
sweeping you flat.

But what if,
like a camel, it's

pure energy I store,
and carry humped and heavy?

Not black, not
that terror, stupidity

of cold rage; or black
only for being pent there?

What if released in air
it became a white

source of light, a fountain
of light? Could all that weight

be the power of flight?
Look inward: see me

with embryo wings, one
feathered in soot, the other

blazing ciliations of ember, pale
flare-pinions. Well—

could I go
on one wing,

the white one?

> You must love the crust of the earth
> on which you dwell. You must be
> able to extract nutriment out of a
> sandheap. You must have so good
> an appetite as this, else you will live
> in vain.
>
> *Thoreau*

Joy, the, 'well . . . *joyfulness* of
joy'—'many years
I had not known it,' the woman of eighty
said, 'only remembered, till now.'

Traherne
in dark fields.
             On Tremont Street,
on the Common, a raw dusk, Emerson
'glad to the brink of fear.'
             It is objective,

stands founded, a roofed gateway;
we cloud-wander

away from it, stumble
again towards it not seeing it,

enter cast-down, discover ourselves
'in joy' as 'in love.'

ii

    'They knocked an
old scar off—the pent blood
rivered out and out—
    When I

white and weak, understood what befell me

speech quickened in me, I
came to myself,'
    —a poet
fifty years old, her look a pool
whose sands have down-spiralled, each grain

dream-clear now, the water
freely itself, visible transparence.

iii

Seeing the locus of joy as the gate
of a city, or as a lych-gate,

I looked up lych-gate: it means
body-gate—here the bearers

rested the bier till the priest came
(to ferry it into a new world).
      'You bring me

life!' Rilke cried to his
deathbed visitor; then, 'Help me

47

towards my death,' then, 'Never forget,
dear one, life is
magnificent!'
                    I looked up 'Joy'
in *Origins,* and came to

'Jubilation' that goes back
to 'a cry of joy or woe' or to 'echoic
iu of wonder.'

iv

Again the old lady
sure for the first time there is a term
to her earth-life

enters the gate—'Joy is
so special a thing, vivid—'

her love for the earth
returns, her heart lightens,
she savors the crust.

Annuals

('Plants that flower the first season
the seed is sown, and then die')

All I planted came up,
balsam and nasturtium and
cosmos and the Marvel of Peru

first the cotyledon
then thickly the differentiated
true leaves of the seedlings,

and I transplanted them,
carefully shaking out each one's
hairfine rootlets from the earth,

and they have thriven,
well-watered in the new-turned earth;
and grow apace now—

but not one shows signs of a flower,
not one.
        If August passes
flowerless,
and the frosts come,

will I have learned to rejoice enough
in the sober wonder of
green healthy leaves?

Those groans men use
passing a woman on the street
or on the steps of the subway

to tell her she is a female
and their flesh knows it,

are they a sort of tune,
an ugly enough song, sung
by a bird with a slit tongue

but meant for music?

Or are they the muffled roaring
of deafmutes trapped in a building that is
slowly filling with smoke?

Perhaps both.

Such men most often
look as if groan were all they could do,
yet a woman, in spite of herself,

knows it's a tribute:
if she were lacking all grace
they'd pass her in silence:

so it's not only to say she's
a warm hole. It's a word

in grief-language, nothing to do with
primitive, not an ur-language;
language stricken, sickened, cast down

in decrepitude. She wants to
throw the tribute away, dis-
gusted, and can't,

it goes on buzzing in her ear,
it changes the pace of her walk,
the torn posters in echoing corridors

spell it out, it
quakes and gnashes as the train comes in.
Her pulse sullenly

had picked up speed,
but the cars slow down and
jar to a stop while her understanding

keeps on translating:
'Life after life after life goes by

without poetry,
without seemliness,
without love.'

The Cat as Cat

The cat on my bosom
sleeping and purring
—fur-petalled chrysanthemum,
squirrel-killer—

is a metaphor only if I
force him to be one,
looking too long in his pale, fond,
dilating, contracting eyes

that reject mirrors, refuse
to observe what bides
stockstill.
         Likewise

flex and reflex of claws
gently pricking through sweater to skin
gently sustains their own tune,
not mine. I-Thou, cat, I-Thou.

Living

The fire in leaf and grass
so green it seems
each summer the last summer.

The wind blowing, the leaves
shivering in the sun,
each day the last day.

A red salamander
so cold and so
easy to catch, dreamily

moves his delicate feet
and long tail. I hold
my hand open for him to go.

Each minute the last minute.

52

A Lamentation

Grief, have I denied thee?
Grief, I have denied thee.

That robe or tunic, black gauze
over black and silver my sister wore
to dance *Sorrow*, hung so long
in my closet. I never tried it on.
                    And my dance
was *Summer*—they rouged my cheeks
and twisted roses with wire stems into my hair.
I was compliant, Juno de sept ans,
betraying my autumn birthright pour faire plaisir.
Always denial. Grief in the morning, washed away
in coffee, crumbled to a dozen errands between
busy fingers.

                    Or across cloistral shadow, insistent
intrusion of pink sunstripes from open
archways, falling recurrent.

Corrosion denied, the figures the acid designs
filled in. Grief dismissed,
and Eros along with grief.
Phantasmagoria swept across the sky
by shaky winds endlessly,
the spaces of blue timidly steady—
blue curtains at trailer windows framing
the cinder walks.
There are hidden corners of sky
choked with the swept shreds, with pain and ashes.
                                        Grief,

have I denied thee? Denied thee.
The emblems torn from the walls,
and the black plumes.

(Olga Levertoff, 1914–1964)

i

By the gas-fire, kneeling
to undress,
scorching luxuriously, raking
her nails over olive sides, the red
waistband ring—

(And the little sister
beady-eyed in the bed—
or drowsy, was I? My head
a camera—)

Sixteen. Her breasts
round, round, and
dark-nippled—

who now these two months long
is bones and tatters of flesh in earth.

ii

The high pitch of
nagging insistence, lines
creased into raised brows—

Ridden, ridden—
the skin around the nails
nibbled sore—

You wanted
to shout the world to its senses,
did you?—to browbeat

the poor into joy's
socialist republic—
What rage

and human shame swept you
when you were nine and saw
the Ley Street houses,

grasping their meaning as *slum*.
Where I, reaching that age,
teased you, admiring

architectural probity, circa
eighteen-fifty, and noted
pride in the whitened doorsteps.

Black one, black one,
there was a white
candle in your heart.

iii

i

Everything flows
                    she muttered into my childhood,
pacing the trampled grass where human puppets
rehearsed fates that summer,
stung into alien semblances by the lash of her will—

everything flows—
I looked up from my Littlest Bear's cane armchair
and knew the words came from a book
and felt them alien to me

but linked to words we loved
                              from the hymnbook—*Time*
like an ever-rolling stream / bears all its sons away—

                    ii

Now as if smoke or sweetness were blown my way
I inhale a sense of her livingness in that instant,
feeling, dreaming, hoping, knowing boredom and zest like anyone
                                                            else

a young girl in the garden, the same alchemical square
I grew in, we thought sometimes
too small for our grand destinies--
                              But dread
was in her, a bloodbeat, it was against the rolling dark
oncoming river she raised bulwarks, setting herself
to sift cinders after early Mass all of one winter,

labelling her desk's normal disorder, basing
her verses on Keble's *Christian Year*, picking
those endless arguments, pressing on

to manipulate lives to disaster . . . To change,
to change the course of the river! What rage for order
disordered her pilgrimage—so that for years at a time

she would hide among strangers, waiting
to rearrange all mysteries in a new light.

Black one, incubus—
     she appeared
riding anguish as Tartars ride mares

over the stubble of bad years.

In one of the years
    when I didn't know if she were dead or alive
I saw her in dream

haggard and rouged
       lit by the flare
from an eel- or cockle-stand on a slum street—

was it a dream? I had lost

all sense, almost, of
    who she was, what—inside of her skin,
under her black hair
              dyed blonde—

it might feel like to be, in the wax and wane of the moon,
in the life I feel as unfolding, not flowing, the pilgrim years—

iv

On your hospital bed you lay
in love, the hatreds
that had followed you, a
comet's tail, burned out

as your disasters bred of love
burned out,
while pain and drugs
quarreled like sisters in you—

lay afloat on a sea
of love and pain—how you always
loved that cadence, 'Underneath
are the everlasting arms'—

all history
burned out, down
to the sick bone, save for

that kind candle.

v

i

In a garden grene whenas I lay—

you set the words to a tune so plaintive
it plucks its way through my life as through a wood.

As through a wood, shadow and light between birches,
gliding a moment in open glades, hidden by thickets of holly

your life winds in me.   In Valentines
a root protrudes from the greensward several yards from its tree

we might raise like a trapdoor's handle, you said,
and descend long steps to another country

where we would live without father or mother
and without longing for the upper world. *The birds
sang sweet,* O song, *in the midst of the daye,*

and we entered silent mid-Essex churches on hot afternoons
and communed with the effigies of knights and their ladies

and their slender dogs asleep at their feet,
the stone so cold—   *In youth*

is pleasure, in youth is pleasure.

ii

Under autumn clouds, under white
wideness of winter skies you went walking
the year you were most alone

returning to the old roads, seeing again
the signposts pointing to Theydon Garnon
or Stapleford Abbots or Greensted,

crossing the ploughlands (whose color I named *murple,*
a shade between brown and mauve that we loved
when I was a child and you

not much more than a child) finding new lanes
near White Roding or Abbess Roding; or lost in Romford's
new streets where there were footpaths then—

frowning as you ground out your thoughts, breathing deep
of the damp still air, taking
the frost into your mind unflinching.

How cold it was in your thin coat, your down-at-heel shoes—
tearless Niobe, your children were lost to you
and the stage lights had gone out, even the empty theater

was locked to you, cavern of transformation where all
had almost been possible.
                                    How many books
you read in your silent lodgings that winter,
how the plovers transpierced your solitude out of doors with their
                                                                    strange cries
I had flung open my arms to in longing, once, by your side
stumbling over the furrows—

Oh, in your torn stockings, with unwaved hair,
you were trudging after your anguish
over the bare fields, soberly, soberly.

vi

Your eyes were the brown gold of pebbles under water.
I never crossed the bridge over the Roding, dividing
the open field of the present from the mysteries,
the wraiths and shifts of time-sense Wanstead Park held suspended,
without remembering your eyes. Even when we were estranged
and my own eyes smarted in pain and anger at the thought of you.
And by other streams in other countries; anywhere where the light
reaches down through shallows to gold gravel. Olga's
brown eyes. One rainy summer, down in the New Forest,
when we could hardly breathe for ennui and the low sky,
you turned savagely to the piano and sightread
straight through all the Beethoven sonatas, day after day—
weeks, it seemed to me. I would turn the pages some of the time,
go out to ride my bike, return—you were enduring in the

falls and rapids of the music, the arpeggios rang out, the rectory
trembled, our parents seemed effaced.
I think of your eyes in that photo, six years before I was born,
the fear in them. What did you do with your fear,
later? Through the years of humiliation,
of paranoia and blackmail and near-starvation, losing
the love of those you loved, one after another,
parents, lovers, children, idolized friends, what kept
compassion's candle alight in you, that lit you
clear into another chapter (but the same book) 'a clearing
in the selva oscura,
a house whose door
swings open, a hand beckons
in welcome'?
                    I cross
so many brooks in the world, there is so much light
dancing on so many stones, so many questions my eyes
smart to ask of your eyes, gold brown eyes,
the lashes short but the lids
arched as if carved out of olivewood, eyes with some vision
of festive goodness in back of their hard, or veiled, or shining,
unknowable gaze. . .

May–August, 1964

NOTE: The quoted lines in the sixth section are an adapta-
tion of some lines in 'Selva Oscura' by the late Louis Mac-
Neice, a poem much loved by my sister.

The Closed World

'If the Perceptive Organs close, their
Objects seem to close also.'
                    Blake: *Jerusalem*

The house-snake dwells here still
under the threshold
but for months I have not seen it
nor its young, the inheritors.

Light and the wind enact
passion and resurrection
day in, day out
but the blinds are down over my windows,
my doors are shut.

When after the long drought at last
silver and darkness swept over the hills
the dry indifferent glare in my mind's eye
wavered but burned on.

Second Didactic Poem

The honey of man is
the task we're set to: to be
'more ourselves'
in the making:
                    'bees of the invisible' working
in cells of flesh and psyche,
filling
        'la grande ruche d'or.'

Nectar,
          the makings of the
incorruptible,
                    is carried upon the
corrupt tongues of
mortal insects,
fanned with their wisps of wing
                    'to evaporate
excess water,'
                    enclosed and capped
with wax, the excretion
of bees' abdominal glands.
Beespittle, droppings, hairs
of beefur: all become honey.
Virulent micro-organisms cannot
survive in honey.
                    The taste,
the odor of honey:
each has no analogue but itself.

In our gathering, in our containing, in our
working, active within ourselves,
slowly the pale
dew-beads of light
lapped up from flowers
can thicken,
darken to gold:

honey of the human.

The disasters numb within us
caught in the chest, rolling
in the brain like pebbles. The feeling
resembles lumps of raw dough

weighing down a child's stomach on baking day.
Or Rilke said it, 'My heart. . .
Could I say of it, it overflows
with bitterness . . . but no, as though

its contents were simply balled into
formless lumps, thus
do I carry it about.'
The same war

continues.
We have breathed the grits of it in, all our lives,
our lungs are pocked with it,
the mucous membrane of our dreams
coated with it, the imagination
filmed over with the gray filth of it:

the knowledge that humankind,

delicate Man, whose flesh
responds to a caress, whose eyes
are flowers that perceive the stars,

whose music excels the music of birds,
whose laughter matches the laughter of dogs,
whose understanding manifests designs
fairer than the spider's most intricate web,

still turns without surprise, with mere regret
to the scheduled breaking open of breasts whose milk
runs out over the entrails of still-alive babies,
transformation of witnessing eyes to pulp-fragments,
implosion of skinned penises into carcass-gulleys.

We are the humans, men who can make;
whose language imagines *mercy,*
lovingkindness; we have believed one another
mirrored forms of a God we felt as good—

who do these acts, who convince ourselves
it is necessary; these acts are done
to our own flesh; burned human flesh
is smelling in Viet Nam as I write.

Yes, this is the knowledge that jostles for space
in our bodies along with all we
go on knowing of joy, of love;

our nerve filaments twitch with its presence
day and night,
nothing we say has not the husky phlegm of it in the saying,
nothing we do has the quickness, the sureness,
the deep intelligence living at peace would have.

To Speak

To speak of sorrow
works upon it
                moves it from its
crouched place barring
the way to and from the soul's hall—

65

out in the light it
shows clear, whether
shrunken or known as
a giant wrath—
                    discrete
at least, where before

its great shadow joined
the walls and roof and seemed
to uphold the hall like a beam.

Bedtime

We are a meadow where the bees hum,
mind and body are almost one

as the fire snaps in the stove
and our eyes close,

and mouth to mouth, the covers
pulled over our shoulders,

we drowse as horses drowse afield,
in accord; though the fall cold

surrounds our warm bed, and though
by day we are singular and often lonely.

Relearning the Alphabet

(June, 1968—April, 1969)

*For G. who could not help it, I. who saw me,
R. who read me, and M. for everything.*

"The treasure . . . lies buried. There is no need
to seek it in a distant country . . . It is behind
the stove, the center of the life and warmth
that rule our existence, if only we knew how to
unearth it. And yet there is this strange and
persistent fact, that it is only after . . . a jour-
ney in a distant region, in a new land, that . . .
the inner voice . . . can make itself understood
by us. And to this strange and persistent fact is
added another: that he who reveals to us the
meaning of our . . . inward pilgrimage must be
himself a stranger . . ."

—*Heinrich Zimmer*

A

Joy—a beginning.   Anguish, ardor.
To relearn the ah! of knowing in unthinking
joy: the belovéd stranger lives.
Sweep up anguish as with a wing-tip,
brushing the ashes back to the fire's core.

B

To be. To love an other only for being.

C

Clear, cool? Not those evasions. The seeing
that burns through, comes through to
the fire's core.

D

In the beginning was delight. A depth
stirred as one stirs fire unthinking.
Dark   dark   dark   . And the blaze illumines
dream.

E

Endless
returning, endless
revolution of dream to ember, ember to anguish,
anguish to flame, flame to delight,
delight to dark and dream, dream to ember

F

that the mind's fire may not fail.
The *vowels of affliction*, of unhealed
not to feel it, uttered,
transformed in utterance
to song.
          Not farewell, not farewell, but faring

G

forth into the grace of transformed
continuance, the green meadows
of Grief-Dale where joy grew, flowering
close to the ground, old tales recount,

H

and may be had yet for the harvesting.

I, J

Into the world of continuance, to find
I-who-I-am again, who wanted
to enter a life not mine,
              to leap a wide, deep, swift river.

At the edge, I stand yet. No, I am moving away,
walking away from the unbridged rush of waters towards
'Imagination's holy forest,' meaning to thread its ways,
                        that are dark,
and come to my own clearing, where 'dreamy, gloomy,
friendly trees' grow, one by one—but
              I'm not looking where I'm going,
              my head's turned back, to see
                   whom I called 'jester': someone dreamed
              on the far bank: not dreamed, seen
in epiphany, as Picasso's bronze *Head of a Jester*
was seen.
         I go stumbling
                   (head turned)
                                  back to my origins:
(if that's where I'm going)
                   to joy, my Jerusalem.
Weeping, gesturing,
I'm a small figure in mind's eye,
diminishing in the sweep of rain or gray tears
that cloud the far shore as jealous rage
clouds love and changes it, changes vision.

K

Caritas is what I must travel to.
Through to the fire's core,
an alchemy:
              caritas, claritas.
But find my face clenched
when I wake at night
                   in limbo.

69

L

Back there forgetting, among the
letters   folded and put away.
Not uttered.
                    'The feel of
not to feel it
was never said . . .' Keats said.
'Desolation . . . Absence an absolute
presence
            calling forth . . .' the jester said
from the far shore ('gravely, ringing his bells,
a tune of sorrow.' I dance to it?)
'You are offhand. The trouble
is concealed?' Isak said,
calling me forth.
I am called forth
from time to time.

I was in the time
of desolation.
What light is it
waking me?
                    Absence has not become
a presence.
            Lost in the alphabet
            I was looking for
            the word I can't now say
(love)
        and am called forth
        unto the twelfth letter
        by the love in a question.

M

Honest man, I wanted
> the moon and went
> out to sea to touch
> the moon and

> down a lane of bright
> broken vanishing
> curled pyramids of
> moonwater
> moving
> towards the moon
and touched
the luminous dissolving
half moon
cold

I am
come back,
humbled, to warm myself,
honest man,

our bed is
> upon the earth
your soul is
> in your body
your mouth
> has found
my mouth once more
—I'm home.

N

Something in me that wants to cling
to *never*,
> wants to have been
> wounded deeper
> burned by the cold moon to cinder,

shrinks as the disk
dwindles to vision

               numb not to continuance
               but to that source
               of mind's fire

               waning now,
               no doubt to wax again—

               yet I perhaps not be there
               in its light.

O

Hostile.   Ordinary.   Home.
Order.   Alone.   Other.

Hostile longing.   Ordinary rose, omnivorous.
           Home, solitude.

Somnolence grotto.
Caught. Lost. Orient almost,
volition.
Own.   Only.

Pain recedes, rising from heart to head
and out.

               Apple thunder, rolling over the
attic floor.

               Yet I would swear
               there had been savage light
               moments before.

P, Q

In childhood dream-play I was always
the knight or squire, not
the lady:
quester, petitioner, win or lose, not
she who was sought.
The initial of quest or question
branded itself long since on the flank
of my Pegasus.
Yet he flies always
home to the present.

R

Released through bars of sorrow
as if not a gate had opened but I
grown intangible had passed through, shadowy,
from dark of yearning into
a soft day, western March;
a thrust of birdsong
parts the gold flowers thickbranching
that roof the path over.

Arms enfold me
tenderly. I am trusted, I trust
the real that transforms me.
                          And relinquish
                          in grief
the seeing that burns through, comes through
to fire's core: transformation, continuance,
                    as acts of magic I would perform, are no longer
                    articles of faith.

S

Or no: it
slowly becomes known to me:
articles of faith are indeed
rules of the will—graceless,
                    faithless.
The door I flung my weight against
was constructed to open   out
                    towards me.

In-seeing
to candleflame's
blue ice-cavern, measureless,

may not be forced by sharp
desire.
          The Prince
          turns in the wood: 'Retrace
                    thy steps, seek out
          the hut you passed, impatient,
          the day you lost your quarry.

          There dwells
          a secret. Restore to it
          its life.
          You will not recognize
          your desire until
          thou hast it fast, it goeth
          aside, it hath
          the cunning of quicksilver.'

I turn in the forest.
About me the tree-multitudes
twist their roots in earth
to rip it, draw

hidden rivers up into
branch-towers.
Their crowns in the light sway
green beyond vision.

                         All utterance
takes me step by hesitant step towards

T

—yes, to continuance: into
                              that life beyond the dead-end where
(in a desert time of
dry strange heat, of dust
that tinged mountain clouds with copper,
turn of the year impending unnoticed,
the cactus shadows brittle thornstars,
time of
desolation)   I was lost.

The forest is holy.
The sacred paths are of stone.
A clearing.
The altars are shifting deposits of pineneedles,
                hidden waters,
                streets of choirwood,
not what the will
thinks to construct for its testimonies.

U

Relearn the alphabet,
relearn the world, the world
understood anew only in doing, under-
stood only as
looked-up-into out of earth,
the heart an eye looking,
the heart a root
planted in earth.
Transmutation is not
under the will's rule.

V

Vision sets out
journeying somewhere,
walking the dreamwaters:
arrives
not on the far shore but upriver,
a place not evoked, discovered.

.

W

Heart breaks but mends
like good bone.
It's the vain will
wants to have been wounded deeper,
burned by the cold moon to cinder.

Wisdom's a stone
dwells in forgotten pockets—
lost, refound, exiled—
revealed again
in the palm of
mind's hand, moonstone
of wax and wane, stone pulse.

Y

Vision will not be used.
Yearning will not be used.
Wisdom will not be used.
Only the vain will
strives to use and be used,
comes not to fire's core
but cinder.

Z

Sweep up
anguish as with a wing-tip:

the blaze addresses
a different darkness:
absence has not become
the transformed presence the will
looked for,
but other: the present,

that which was poised already in the ah! of praise.

The Broken Sandal

Dreamed the thong of my sandal broke.
Nothing to hold it to my foot.
How shall I walk?
          Barefoot?
The sharp stones, the dirt. I would
hobble.
And—
Where was I going?
Where was I going I can't
go to now, unless hurting?
Where am I standing, if I'm
to stand still now?

77

i

Twenty years, forty years, it's nothing.
Not a mirage; the blink
of an eyelid.

Life is nibbling us with little
lips, circling our knees, our
shoulders.
            What's the difference,
a kiss or a fin-caress. Only sometimes
the water reddens,
we ebb.

Birth, marriage, death, we've had them,
checked them off on our list,
and still stand here

tiptoe on the mud,
half-afloat,
water up to the neck.

It's a big pond.

ii

What do I know?
            Swing of the
            birch catkins,
            drift of
            watergrass,
            tufts of
            green on the
            trees,

                    (flowers, not leaves,
                    bearing intricately
                    little winged seeds
                    to fly in fall)
                    and whoever
                    I meet now,
                    on the path.
It's not enough.

iii

Biology and the computer—
the speaker implies
we're obsolescent,

we who grew up
towards utopias.

In this
amnesia of the heart
I'm wondering,

I almost believe him.
What do I know?
A poem, turn of the head,

some certainty
of mordant delight—
five notes, the return
of the All Day Bird—:

truces, for the new moon
or the spring solstice,
and at midnight the firing resumes,

far away.
It's not real.

We wanted
more of our life to live in us.
To imagine each other.

iv

Twenty years, forty years,
'to live in the present' was a utopia
moved towards

in tears, stumbling, falling,
getting up, going on—
and now the arrival,

the place of pilgrimage curiously
open, not, it turns out,
a circle of holy stones,

no altar, no
high peak,
no deep valley, the world's navel,

but a plain,
only green tree-flowers
thinly screening the dayglare

and without silence—
we hear the traffic, the highway's
only a stonesthrow away.

Is this the place?

v

This is not the place.
The spirit's left it.

Back to that mud my feet felt
when as a child I fell off a bridge
and almost drowned, but rising

found myself dreamily upright,
water sustaining me,
my hair watergrass.

vi

Fishes bare their teeth to our flesh.
The sky's drifting toward our mouths.
Forty years redden the spreading circles.
Blink of an eyelid,
nothing,
obsolete future—

vii

If I should find my poem is deathsongs.
If I find it has ended, when
I looked for the next step.

Not Spring is unreal to me,
I have the tree-flowers by heart.
Love, twenty years, forty years, my life,
        is unreal to me.
I love only the stranger
coming to meet me now
up the path that's pinpricked with
yellow fallen crumbs of pollen.

I who am not about to die,
I who carry my life about with me openly,
health excellent, step light, cheerful, hungry,

my starwheel rolls. Stops
on the point of sight.
Reduced to an eye
I forget what
                    I
was.

Asking the cold spring
what if my poem is deathsongs.

At David's Grave

for B. and H. F.

Yes, he is here in this
open field, in sunlight, among
the few young trees set out
to modify the bare facts—

he's here, but only
because we are here.
When we go, he goes with us

to be your hands that never
do violence, your eyes
that wonder, your lives

that daily praise life
by living it, by laughter.

He is never alone here,
never cold in the field of graves.

What Wild Dawns There Were

What wild dawns there were
    in our first years here
when we would run outdoors naked
to pee in the long grass behind the house
        and see over the hills such streamers,
        such banners of fire and blue (the blue
        that is Lilith to full day's honest Eve)—
What feathers of gold under the morning star
    we saw from dazed eyes before
stumbling back to bed chilled with dew
to sleep till the sun was high!

Now if we wake early
    we don't go outdoors—or I don't—
    and you if you do go
    rarely call me to see the day break.
I watch the dawn through glass: this year
        only cloudless flushes of light, paleness
        slowly turning to rose,
        and fading subdued.
We have not spoken of these tired
risings of the sun.

Topmost leaves of young oak,
    young maple,
        are red—a delicate red
almost maroon.

I am not young,
    and not yet old. Young enough not to be able
        to imagine my own old age. Something in me

puts out new leaves that are red also,
    delicate, fantastic, in June,
        early summer, late spring in the north.

A dark time we live in. One would think
    there would be no summer. No red leaves.
        One would think there would be

no drawings-up of the blind at morning
    to a field awake with flowers.
        Yet with my tuft of new leaves

it is that field I wake to,
    a woman foolish with desire.

A Cloak

'For there's more enterprise
In walking naked.'
W. B. Yeats

And I walked naked
from the beginning

breathing in
my life,
breathing out
poems,

arrogant in innocence.

But of the song-clouds my breath made
in cold air

a cloak has grown,
white and,
            where here a word
                there another
froze, glittering,
stone-heavy.

A mask I had not meant
to wear, as if of frost,
covers my face.
                Eyes looking out,
a longing silent at song's core.

White dawn. Stillness.   When the rippling began
    I took it for sea-wind, coming to our valley with rumors
    of salt, of treeless horizons. But the white fog
didn't stir; the leaves of my brothers remained outstretched,
unmoving.
            Yet the rippling drew nearer—and then
my own outermost branches began to tingle, almost as if
fire had been lit below them, too close, and their twig-tips
were drying and curling.
                    Yet I was not afraid, only
                    deeply alert.

I was the first to see him, for I grew
            out on the pasture slope, beyond the forest.
He was a man, it seemed: the two
moving stems, the short trunk, the two
arm-branches, flexible, each with five leafless
                    twigs at their ends,
and the head that's crowned by brown or gold grass,
bearing a face not like the beaked face of a bird,
        more like a flower's.
                    He carried a burden made of
some cut branch bent while it was green,
strands of a vine tight-stretched across it. From this,
when he touched it, and from his voice
which unlike the wind's voice had no need of our
leaves and branches to complete its sound,
                    came the ripple.
But it was now no longer a ripple (he had come near and
stopped in my first shadow) it was a wave that bathed me
         as if rain
                rose from below and around me
             instead of falling.
And what I felt was no longer a dry tingling:

I seemed to be singing as he sang, I seemed to know
what the lark knows; all my sap
            was mounting towards the sun that by now
                had risen, the mist was rising, the grass
was drying, yet my roots felt music moisten them
deep under earth.

            He came still closer, leaned on my trunk:
            the bark thrilled like a leaf still-folded.
Music! There was no twig of me not
                                trembling with joy and fear.

Then as he sang
it was no longer sounds only that made the music:
he spoke, and as no tree listens I listened, and language
            came into my roots
                                out of the earth,
                into my bark
                                out of the air,
                into the pores of my greenest shoots
                                gently as dew
and there was no word he sang but I knew its meaning.
He told of journeys,
            of where sun and moon go while we stand in dark,
    of an earth-journey he dreamed he would take some day
deeper than roots . . .
He told of the dreams of man, wars, passions, griefs,
            and I, a tree, understood words—ah, it seemed
my thick bark would split like a sapling's that
                                grew too fast in the spring
when a late frost wounds it.

                                Fire he sang,
that trees fear, and I, a tree, rejoiced in its flames.
New buds broke forth from me though it was full summer.
            As though his lyre (now I knew its name)
            were both frost and fire, its chords flamed
up to the crown of me.

I was seed again.
                    I was fern in the swamp.
                              I was coal.

And at the heart of my wood
(so close I was to becoming man or a god)
          there was a kind of silence, a kind of sickness,
                something akin to what men call boredom,
                                                  something
(the poem descended a scale, a stream over stones)
                that gives to a candle a coldness
                      in the midst of its burning, he said.

It was then,
            when in the blaze of his power that
                              reached me and changed me
            I thought I should fall my length,
that the singer began
                        to leave me.   Slowly
                  moved from my noon shadow
                                          to open light,
words leaping and dancing over his shoulders
back to me
                  rivery sweep of lyre-tones becoming
slowly again
            ripple.

And I
            in terror
                  but not in doubt of
                                    what I must do
in anguish, in haste,
                  wrenched from the earth root after root,
the soil heaving and cracking, the moss tearing asunder—
and behind me the others: my brothers
forgotten since dawn. In the forest
they too had heard,

and were pulling their roots in pain
out of a thousand years' layers of dead leaves,
     rolling the rocks away,
          breaking themselves
                out of
                their depths.
You would have thought we would lose the sound of the lyre,
      of the singing
so dreadful the storm-sounds were, where there was no storm,
     no wind but the rush of our
      branches moving, our trunks breasting the air.
      But the music!
           The music reached us.

Clumsily,
     stumbling over our own roots,
          rustling our leaves
           in answer,
we moved, we followed.

All day we followed, up hill and down.
         We learned to dance,
for he would stop, where the ground was flat,
        and words he said
taught us to leap and to wind in and out
around one another   in figures   the lyre's measure designed.
The singer
     laughed till he wept to see us, he was so glad.
         At sunset
we came to this place I stand in, this knoll
with its ancient grove that was bare grass then.
    In the last light of that day his song became
farewell.
    He stilled our longing.
    He sang our sun-dried roots back into earth,
watered them: all-night rain of music so quiet

                                                    we could almost
                        not hear it in the
                                        moonless dark.
By dawn he was gone.
                        We have stood here since,
in our new life.
                        We have waited.
                                        He does not return.
It is said he made his earth-journey, and lost
what he sought.
                        It is said they felled him
and cut up his limbs for firewood.
                                        And it is said
his head still sang and was swept out to sea singing.
Perhaps he will not return.
                                        But what we have lived
comes back to us.
                        We see more.
                                        We feel, as our rings increase,
something that lifts our branches, that stretches our furthest
                                                            leaf-tips
further.
                        The wind, the birds,
                                        do not sound poorer but clearer,
recalling our agony, and the way we danced.
The music!

Because in Vietnam the vision of a Burning Babe
is multiplied, multiplied,
                              the flesh on fire
not Christ's, as Southwell saw it, prefiguring
the Passion upon the Eve of Christmas,

but wholly human and repeated, repeated,
infant after infant, their names forgotten,
their sex unknown in the ashes,
set alight, flaming but not vanishing,
not vanishing as his vision but lingering,

cinders upon the earth or living on
moaning and stinking in hospitals three abed;

because of this my strong sight,
my clear caressive sight, my poet's sight I was given
that it might stir me to song,
is blurred.
              There is a cataract filming over
my inner eyes. Or else a monstrous insect
has entered my head, and looks out
from my sockets with multiple vision,

seeing not the unique Holy Infant
burning sublimely, an imagination of redemption,
furnace in which souls are wrought into new life,
but, as off a beltline, more, more senseless figures aflame.

And this insect (who is not there—
it is my own eyes do my seeing, the insect
is not there, what I see is there)
will not permit me to look elsewhere,

or if I look, to see except dulled and unfocused
the delicate, firm, whole flesh of the still unburned.

Tenebrae

(Fall of 1967)

Heavy, heavy, heavy, hand and heart.
We are at war,
bitterly, bitterly at war.

And the buying and selling
buzzes at our heads, a swarm
of busy flies, a kind of innocence.

Gowns of gold sequins are fitted,
sharp-glinting. What harsh rustlings
of silver moiré there are,
to remind me of shrapnel splinters.

And weddings are held in full solemnity
not of desire but of etiquette,
the nuptial pomp of starched lace;
a grim innocence.

And picnic parties return from the beaches
burning with stored sun in the dusk;
children promised a TV show when they get home
fall asleep in the backs of a million station wagons,
sand in their hair, the sound of waves
quietly persistent at their ears.
They are not listening.

Their parents at night
dream and forget their dreams.
They wake in the dark
and make plans. Their sequin plans
glitter into tomorrow.
They buy, they sell.

They fill freezers with food.
Neon signs flash their intentions
into the years ahead.

And at their ears the sound
of the war. They are
not listening, not listening.

From STAYING ALIVE

Entr'acte

i   At the Justice Department
      November 15, 1969

Brown gas-fog, white
beneath the street lamps.
Cut off on three sides, all space filled
with our bodies.
        Bodies that stumble
in brown airlessness, whitened
in light, a mildew glare,
        that stumble
hand in hand, blinded, retching.
Wanting it, wanting
to be here, the body believing it's
dying in its nausea, my head
clear in its despair, a kind of joy,
knowing this is by no means death,

is trivial, an incident, a
fragile instant.   Wanting it, wanting
        with all my hunger this anguish,
        this knowing in the body
the grim odds we're
up against, wanting it real.
Up that bank where gas
curled in the ivy, dragging each other
up, strangers, brothers
and sisters.   Nothing
will do but
to taste the bitter
taste. No life
other, apart from.

ii   Gandhi's Gun (and Brecht's Vow)

Vessels of several
shapes and sizes—

bowls, pots,
a tall vase

and the guitar's
waiting body:

forms drawn
by a hand's
energy.

                'Never

            run away from the stormcenter.

                Cultivate

            cool courage, die without killing—'

Strong orange, deep
oil-pastel green

but at the center, strange
upstroke of black

stronger, deeper
than all.
    —'but if one has not

      that courage'—

(or singing, '*Keiner
oder Alle, Alles
oder Nichts!*')
     —'cultivate

   the art of killing and being killed

  rather than in a cowardly manner

    to flee from danger.'

Vessels, counterparts
of the human; primal
vessel of music

towards which like a rifle
that harsh stroke blackly
points upward

would fail, fall from their whirling
dance, without

the terror patiently
poised there,

ultimate focus.

'Let Us Sing Unto the Lord a New Song'

There's a pulse in Richard
that day and night says
revolution   revolution   revolution

and another
not always heard:

poetry   poetry

rippling through his sleep,
a river pulse.

Heart's fire
breaks the chest almost,
flame-pulse,
revolution:

and if its beat
falter
life itself
shall cease.

Heart's river,
living water,
poetry:

and if that pulse
grow faint
fever shall parch the soul, breath
choke upon ashes.

But when their rhythms
mesh
then though the pain of living
never lets up

the singing begins.

Love Poem

for Mitch

Swimming through dark, slow,
breaststroke—
        not to startle
        walls or chairs and
        wake you—
I almost sundered the
full to the brim with moonlight
mirror

September, 1969

for Kenneth Rexroth

Warm wind, the leaves
rustling without dryness,
hills dissolved into silver.

It could be any age,
four hundred years ago or a time
of post-revolutionary peace,
the rivers clean again, birth rate and crops
somehow in balance . . .

In heavy dew
under the moon the blond grasses
lean in swathes on the field slope. Fervently
the crickets practice their religion of ectasy.

The Wanderer

The chameleon who wistfully
thought it could not suffer
nostalgia

now on a vast sheet of clear glass
cowers, and prays for vision
of russet bark and trembling foliage.

The Old King

for Jim Forest

The Soul's dark Cottage, batter'd and decay'd,
Lets in new Light through chinks that Time hath made.

And at night—
the whole night a cavern, the world
an abyss—

lit from within:

a red glow
throbbing at the chinks.

Far-off a wanderer
unhoused, unhouseled,
wonders to see
hearthblaze:
fears, and takes heart.

To stay perhaps,

      one throat far-off
      pulsing to venture
      one note from its feathers,
      one bell,

on into dewfall, into
peculiar silence.

The multitude gone, labyrinths
crumbling.
        To go down
back into the known hole.

Memories of John Keats

for Mitch

Watchfulness and sensation as John Keats
said to me
for it was to me
he said it
            (and to you)

Side by side we lay full-length
upon a spumy rock, envisioning
Ailsa Craig

                    The sea tumult
bore away
            a word
      and a word

And again *that which is creative*
must create itself   he said
We skirted
the murmurous green hollow
Vale of Health

strolling the spiral road, the
Vale of Soulmaking

He would stop to pluck
a leaf, finger
a stone

watchfulness was his word
sensation
            and watchfulness in itself
the Genius
of Poetry must work out
its own salvation in a man

I leapt   he said
headlong into the sea. . .

To Antonio Machado

Here in the mountain woods
a furious small fountain
is channelled through pipes of hollow sapling
into a great wooden vat bevelled with moss,
and thence brims over into a concrete cistern
and from the cistern quietly
in modest rills
into the meadow where cows graze
and fringed wild carnations, white and sweet,
grow by the path.
Machado,
       old man,
              dead man,
       I wish you were here alive
to drink of the cold, earthtasting, faithful spring,
to receive the many voices
of this one brook,
to see its dances
of fury and gentleness,
to write the austere poem
you would have known in it.

Brunnenburg, 1971

The Life around Us

for David Mitchell and David Hass

Poplar and oak awake
all night. And through
all weathers of the days of the year.
There is a consciousness

undefined.
Yesterday's twilight, August
almost over, lasted, slowly changing,
until daybreak. Human sounds
were shut behind curtains.
No human saw the night in this garden,
sliding blue into morning.
Only the sightless trees,
without braincells, lived it
and wholly knew it.

Living Alone   (I)

In this silvery now of living alone,
doesn't it seem, I ponder,
anything can happen?
On the flat roof of a factory
at eye level from my window,
starling naiads dip in tremulous rainpools
where the sky floats, and is no smaller
than long ago.
Any strange staircase, as if I were twenty-one–
any hand drawing me up it,
could lead me to my life.
Some days.

And if I coast, down toward home, spring evenings, silently,
a kind of song rising in me to encompass
Davis Square and the all-night
cafeteria and the pool hall,
it is childhood's song, surely no note is changed,
sung in Valentines Park or on steep streets in the map of my mind
in the hush of suppertime, everyone gone indoors.
Solitude within multitude seduced me early.

Some days, though,
living alone,
there's only knowledge of silence,
clutter of bells cobwebbed
in crumbling belfry,
words jaggéd,
in midutterance broken.

Starlings, as before,
whistle wondering at themselves,
crescendo, diminuendo.
My heart pounds away,
confident as a clock.
Yet there is silence.

New leafed, the neighbor trees
round out. There's one,
near my window,
seems to have no buds, though.

Living Alone   (III)

I said, the summer garden I planted
bears only leaves–leaves in abundance–
but no flowers.
And then the flowers,
        many colors and forms,
        subtle, mysterious,
came forth.

I said, the tree has no buds.
And then the leaves,
        shyly, sparse, as if reluctant,

in less than two days appeared,
and the tree, now,
    is flying on green wings.

What magic denial
shall my life utter
to bring itself forth?

Divorcing

One garland
of flowers, leaves, thorns
was twined round our two necks.
Drawn tight, it could choke us,
yet we loved its scratchy grace,
our fragrant yoke.

We were Siamese twins.
Our blood's not sure
if it can circulate,
now we are cut apart.
Something in each of us is waiting
to see if we can survive,
severed.

Raising our glasses, smilingly
we wish one another not luck
but happiness. After half a lifetime
with and without luck,
we know we need more than luck.
It makes no difference that we're drinking
tomato juice, not wine or whiskey–
we know what we mean,
and the red juice of those virtuous
vegetable-fruits is something we both enjoy.
I remember your wonder, as at a miracle,
finding them growing on sturdy vines
in my old aunt and uncle's sun-room
ripe to pluck at the breakfast table!
We were twenty-three, and unappeasably hungry . . .

We agree on tomatoes, then–and happiness?
yes, that too: we mean growth, branching,
leafing, yielding blossoms and fruit and the sharp odor
                                        of dreams.
We mean knowing someone as deeply,
no, deeper, than we've known each other,
we mean being known. We are wishing each other
the luck not to need luck. I mill
some pepper into my juice, though,
and salt in the ancient gesture; and what would be wrong
with tipping out half a glass
for the gods?
                    We smile.
After these months of pain we begin
to admit our new lives have begun.

February 1975

That a woman not ask a man to leave meaningful work to
                                                    follow her.
That a man not ask a woman to leave meaningful work to
                                                    follow him.

That no one try to put Eros in bondage.
But that no one put a cudgel in the hands of Eros.

That our loyalty to one another and our loyalty to our work
not be set in false conflict.

That our love for each other give us love for each other's work.
That our love for each other's work give us love for one another.

That our love for each other's work give us love for one another.
That our love for each other give us love for each other's work.

That our love for each other, if need be,
give way to absence. And the unknown.

That we endure absence, if need be,
without losing our love for each other.
Without closing our doors to the unknown.

The Freeing of the Dust

Unwrap the dust from its mummycloths.
Let Ariel learn
a blessing for Caliban
and Caliban drink dew from the lotus
open upon the waters.
Bitter the slow
river water: dew
shall wet his lips with light.
Let the dust
float, the wrappings too
are dust.
      Drift upon the stir
of air, of dark
river: ashes of what had lived,
         or seeds
      of ancient sesame,
        or namelessly
pure dust that is all
in all.   Bless,
weightless Spirit. Drink,
Caliban, push your tongue
heavy into the calyx.

It is the one in homespun
you hunger for
when you are lonesome;

the one in crazy feathers
dragging opal chains in dust
wearies you

wearies herself perhaps
but has to drive on
clattering rattletrap into

fiery skies for trophies,
into the blue that is bluer
because of the lamps,

the silence keener because it is solitude
moving through multitude on the night streets.

But the one in homespun
whom you want is weary
too, wants to sit down

beside you neither silent
nor singing, in quietness. Alas,
they are not two but one,

pierce the flesh of one, the other
halfway across the world, will shriek,
her blood will run. Can you endure
life with two brides, bridegroom?

The Life of Others

Their high pitched baying
as if in prayer's unison

remote, undistracted, given over
utterly to belief,

the skein of geese
voyages south,
             hierarchic arrow of its convergence toward
                the point of grace
swinging and rippling, ribbon tail
of a kite, loftily

over lakes where they have not
elected to rest,

over men who suppose
earth is man's, over golden earth

preparing itself
for night and winter.
                  We humans
are smaller than they, and crawl
unnoticed,

about and about the smoky map.

When she cannot be sure
which of two lovers it was with whom she felt
this or that moment of pleasure, of something fiery
streaking from head to heels, the way the white
flame of a cascade streaks a mountainside
seen from a car across a valley, the car
changing gear, skirting a precipice,
climbing . . .
When she can sit or walk for hours after a movie
talking earnestly and with bursts of laughter
with friends, without worrying
that it's late, dinner at midnight, her time
spent without counting the change . . .
When half her bed is covered with books
and no one is kept awake by the reading light
and she disconnects the phone, to sleep till noon . . .
Then
selfpity dries up, a joy
untainted by guilt lifts her.
She has fears, but not about loneliness;
fears about how to deal with the aging
of her body—how to deal
with photographs and the mirror. She feels
so much younger and more beautiful
than she looks. At her happiest
—or even in the midst of
some less than joyful hour, sweating
patiently through a heatwave in the city
or hearing the sparrows at daybreak, dully gray,
toneless, the sound of fatigue—
a kind of sober euphoria makes her believe
in her future as an old woman, a wanderer,
seamed and brown,
little luxuries of the middle of life all gone,
watching cities and rivers, people and mountains,

without being watched; not grim nor sad,
an old winedrinking woman, who knows
the old roads, grass-grown, and laughs to herself . . .
She knows it can't be:
that's Mrs. Doasyouwouldbedoneby from

The Water-Babies,

no one can walk the world any more,
a world of fumes and decibels.
But she thinks maybe
she could get to be tough and wise, some way,
anyway. Now at least
she is past the time of mourning,
now she can say without shame or deceit,
O blessed Solitude.

Chekhov on the West Heath

for Jim McConkey
who spurred me into writing it
and for Rebecca Garnett
who was and is 'Bet'

A young girl in a wheelchair,
another girl pushing the chair.
Up from Heath Mansions they go,
past the long brick wall of the Fenton House garden.
The invalid girl's hands move as she speaks, delicately,
describing the curve of a cloud.
The other, younger one comes into focus;
how could I know so well
the back of my own head? I could touch the hair
of the long plait . . . Ah,
that's it: the young girl painting
in Corot's *L'Atelier*, upright, absorbed,
whose face we don't see. *There I am,*
I thought, the first time I saw it,
startled.
Up through small streets they go,
the crest of the hill, a stonesthrow of unpaved lane,
and out to the terrace: a few
lopsided benches, tussocky grass,
and the great billowing prospect north.
This is Hampstead. This
is Judge's Walk. It is nineteen hundred
and forty-one.
The war? They take it for granted;
it was predicted while they were children,
and has come to pass. It means
no more ballet school, Betty is ill,
I am beginning to paint in oils.
The war is simply

112

how the world is, to which they were born.
They share
 the epiphanies of their solitudes,
hardly knowing or speaking to anyone else
their own age. They have not discovered men
or sex at all. But daily
they live! Live
intensely. Mysterious fragrance
gentles the air
under the black poplars.
And Bet, looking off towards hawthorn and willow,
middle-distance of valley and steep small hills,
says she would like to bounce
from one round-topped tree to another,
in the spring haze.

Often and often, as they talk and gaze,
that year and the next,
                              Chekhov is with them.
With us.
        The small, dark-green volumes.
        The awkward, heroic versions.
We're not systematic,
we don't even *try* to read all of them, held secure
in conviction of endless largesse.

                              Bet's glinting hair
in tendrils around her face. Her hands
thin. A spirit
woven of silk, has grown in her, as if bodily strength,
dwindling, had been a cocoon,
                        and only by this strange weakness
could her intelligence be freed, that instructs
the poet in me.
Alone at home, in between visits, I write, paint,
read and read, practice *Für Elise* with feeling
                              (and too much pedal)
help with the housework or shirk it,
and wait.

What did he say to us, Chekhov? Who was this Chekhov
pacing the round of the Whitestone Pond,
his hand on the chair coming down Heath Street,
telling the tale of Kashtanka in the gloomy sickroom
back at Heath Mansions?
                              Ah, even though
the dark gauze of youth
swaddled us,
                    while airraids and news of battle
were part of each ominous day, and in flashes of dread
we glimpsed invasion, England and Europe gone down
utterly into the nightmare;
                              even though Bet
was fading, month by month, and no one knew why–
we were open to life and hope: it was that he gave us,
generous, precise, lifting us
into the veins of a green leaf, translucent,
setting our hearts' tinder alight,
                              sun striking on glass to release
the latent flames.

When the Black Monk
swiftly drew near, a whirlwind column grown
                              from a pinpoint
to giant size, then–shrinking to human measure,
and passing inaudibly–moved through the solid trees
to vanish like smoke,
                              we thrilled to the presence of a power,
unquestioning. We knew
everything and nothing, nothing and everything.
Glimpsing a verity we could not define,
we saw that the story is not about illusion,
it's about what is true: 'the great garden
     with its miraculous flowers,
     the pines with their shaggy roots,
     the ryefield, marvellous science, youth,
     daring, joy . . .' That was the Chekhov we knew.

And the betrothed girl, who listens and listens
to a different and useful life calling her, and *does*

114

wrench herself free and go to study—and more,
comes back and *again* frees herself, journeying forth
(because a man dying, who himself
could not be free, gave her
his vision) into the hard, proto-revolutionary future,
her step forward for all of us,
as his words were for her—she was the Chekhov
who slipped unrecognized into our dreaming days.
She was at Bet's side when Bet,
a woman with grown children, so changed
from the girl in the wheelchair, a woman alone
with years of struggle behind her, sturdy—
yet still afraid—began, in spite of her fear,
to learn to teach. And at *my* side
in Berkeley, Boston, Washington, when we held our line
before advancing troopers, or sang out, 'Walk,
don't run,' retreating from gas and billyclubs,

                                     trying to learn
to act in the world.
                  She, The Betrothed,
whose marriage was not with her fiancé but with her life's
need to grow, to work for Chekhov's
    'Holy of holies—the human body, health, intelligence,
    inspiration, love,
    and the most absolute
    freedom from violence and lying'—she
was the Chekhov we knew.

                        What he would mean to us
we still can know only in part. (What has the Heath,
which Bet has lived close to always, and I,
through decades away, never quite lost sight of,
meant in our lives? A place of origin
gives and gives, as we return to it,
bringing our needs.) What he has meant
and goes on meaning, can't be trapped
into closed definition. But it has to do
not with failure, defeat, frustration,
Moscows never set out for,

but with love.
                          The sharp steel
of his scorn for meanness and cruelty gleamed
over our sheltered heads only half-noticed,
and irony was beyond our grasp,
we couldn't laugh with him; nevertheless
some inkling of rectitude and compassion
came to us, breathed in
under the fragrant leaves in wartime London, to endure
somewhere throughout the tumult of years. How,
                                              in our crude,
vague, dreamy ignorance could we recognize
              'the subtle, elusive beauty of human grief'?
Yet from between the dark green bindings
it rose, wafting into us, ready
to bide its time. The man who imagined a ring
inscribed with the words, 'Nothing passes,'
that rich man's son whom the townsfolk called
                                              'Small Gain,'
who suffered loss after loss, and was
                                       'left with the past,'
he too—for beyond despair
he carried in him the seed of change, the vision,
seeing not only *what is* but *what might be*—
he too was the Chekhov we knew, unknowing.

                          As we looked out
into the haze from that open height
familiar to Keats and Constable in their day—
a place built not only of earth but of layers
of human response, little hill
in time, in history—
your smile, Chekhov, 'tender, delightful, ironic,'
looked over our shoulders; and still looks, now,
half of our lifetime gone by, or more,
till we turn to see
who you were, who you are, everpresent, vivid,
luminous dust.

The 90th Year

for Lore Segal

High in the jacaranda shines the gilded thread
of a small bird's curlicue of song–too high
for her to see or hear.
                    I've learned
not to say, these last years,
'O, look!–O, listen, Mother!'
as I used to.

            (It was she
who taught me to look;
to name the flowers when I was still close to the ground,
my face level with theirs;
or to watch the sublime metamorphoses
unfold and unfold
over the walled back gardens of our street . . .

It had not been given her
to know the flesh as good in itself,
as the flesh of a fruit is good. To her
the human body has been a husk,
a shell in which souls were prisoned.
Yet, from within it, with how much gazing
her life has paid tribute to the world's body!
How tears of pleasure
would choke her, when a perfect voice,
deep or high, clove to its note unfaltering!)

She has swept the crackling seedpods,
the litter of mauve blossoms, off the cement path,
tipped them into the rubbish bucket.
She's made her bed, washed up the breakfast dishes,
wiped the hotplate. I've taken the butter and milkjug
back to the fridge next door–but it's not my place,

117

visiting here, to usurp the tasks
that weave the day's pattern.
Now she is leaning forward in her chair,
            by the lamp lit in the daylight,
rereading *War and Peace*.
                        When I look up
from her wellworn copy of *The Divine Milieu*,
which she wants me to read, I see her hand
loose on the black stem of the magnifying glass,
she is dozing.
'I am so tired,' she has written to me, 'of appreciating
the gift of life.'

A Soul-Cake

Mother, when I open a book of yours
your study notes fall out into my lap.
'Apse, semicircular or polygonal recess
arched over domed roof,' says one. I remember
your ceiling, cracked by earthquake,
and left that way. Not that you chose to leave it;
nevertheless, 'There's nothing less real
than the present,' you underlined.

My throat clenches when I weep and
can't make tears,
the way my feet clenched when I ran
unsuspecting into icy ocean
for 'General swim,' visiting Nik at summercamp.
What hurts is not your absence only,
dull, unresonant, final,
it's the intimate knowledge of your aspirations,
the scholar in you, the artist reaching
out and out.
            To strangers your unremitting
struggle to learn appears

a triumph—to me, poignant. I know
how baffled you felt.
I know only I
knew how lonely you were.
The small orphan,
skinny, proud, reserved, observant,
irreverent still in the woman of ninety,
but humble.

"To force conscience," you marked in Panofsky,
"is worse,' says Castellio, 'than cruelly
to kill a man. For to deny one's convictions
destroys the soul."
              And Bruno's lines,
"The age
Which I have lived, live, and shall live,
Sets me atremble, shakes, and braces me."

Five months before you died you recalled
counting-rhymes, dance-games for me;
gaily, under the moon, you sang and mimed,

                   My shoes are very *dir*ty,
                   My shoes are very *thin,*
                   I haven't got a *poc*ket
                   To put a penny in.

                   A soul-cake, a soul-cake,
                   Please, good missis, a soul-cake . . .

But by then for two years
you had hardly been able to hear me,
could barely see to read.
               We spoke together
               less and less.

There's too much grief. Mother,
what shall I do with it?
Salt grinding and grinding from the magic box.

Ah, grief, I should not treat you
like a homeless dog
who comes to the back door
for a crust, for a meatless bone.
I should trust you.

I should coax you
into the house and give you
your own corner,
a worn mat to lie on,
your own water dish.

You think I don't know you've been living
under my porch.
You long for your real place to be readied
before winter comes. You need
your name,
your collar and tag. You need
the right to warn off intruders,
to consider
my house your own
and me your person
and yourself
my own dog.

My wedding-ring lies in a basket
as if at the bottom of a well.
Nothing will come to fish it back up
and onto my finger again.
                              It lies
among keys to abandoned houses,
nails waiting to be needed and hammered
into some wall,
telephone numbers with no names attached,
idle paperclips.
                    It can't be given away
for fear of bringing ill-luck.
                    It can't be sold
for the marriage was good in its own
time, though that time is gone.
                    Could some artificer
beat into it bright stones, transform it
into a dazzling circlet no one could take
for solemn betrothal or to make promises
living will not let them keep? Change it
into a simple gift I could give in friendship?

Try to remember, every April, not this one only
you feel you are walking underwater
in a lake stained by your blood.

When the east wind rips the sunlight
your neck feels thin and weak, your clothes
don't warm you.

You feel you are lurching away from
deft shears, rough hands, your fleece
lies at the shepherd's feet.

And in the first warm days each step
pushes you against a weight,
and you don't want

to resist that weight,
you want to stop, to return
to darkness
                    —but treaties made
over your head force you to
waver forward.

Yes, this year you feel
at a loss, there is no Demeter
to whom to return

if for a moment you saw
yourself as Persephone.
It is she, Demeter, has gone
                down to the dark.

Or if it is Orpheus drawing you forth,
Eurydice,
he is inexorable, and does not look back
to let you go.

You are appalled to consider you may be destined
to live to a hundred.
But it is April,

there is nothing unique in your losses,
your pain is commonplace
and your road ordained:

your steps will hurt you,
you will arrive
as usual

at some condition you name *summer*:

> an ample landscape,
> voluptuous, calm,
> of large, very still trees,
> water meadows, dreamy
> savannah distances,

where you will gather strength,
pulling ripe fruit from the boughs,
for winter and spring,
forgotten seasons.

Try to remember it is always this way.
You live
this April's pain
now,

you will come
to other Aprils,
each will astonish you.

I send my messages ahead of me.
You read them, they speak to you
in siren tongues, ears of flame
spring from your heads to take them.

When I arrive, you love me,
for I sing those messages you've
leaned by heart, and bring,
as housegifts, new ones. You hear
yourselves in them,
self after self. Your solitudes
utter their runes, your own
voices begin to rise in your throats.

But soon you love me less.
I brought with me
too much, too many laden coffers,
the panoply of residence,

improper to a visit.
Silks and furs, my enormous wings,
my crutches, and my spare crutches,
my desire to please, and worse–

my desire to judge what is right.

I take up
so much space.
You are living on what you can find,
you don't want charity, and you can't
support lingering guests.

When I leave, I leave
alone, as I came.

The Dragonfly-Mother

I was setting out from my house
to keep my promise

but the Dragonfly-Mother stopped me.

I was to speak to a multitude
for a good cause, but at home

the Dragonfly-Mother was listening
not to a speech but to the creak of
                    stretching tissue,
tense hum of leaves unfurling.

Who is the Dragonfly-Mother?
What does she do?

She is the one who hovers
on stairways of air,
                    sometimes almost
grazing your cheekbone,
she is the one who darts unforeseeably
into unsuspected dimensions,

who sees in water
her own blue fire zigzag, and lifts
her self in laughter
into the tearful pale sky

that sails blurred clouds in the stream.

•

She sat at my round table,
we told one another dreams,
I stayed home breaking my promise.

When she left I slept
three hours, and arose

and wrote. I remember the cold
Waterwoman, in dragonfly dresses

and blue shoes, long ago.
She is the same,

whose children were thin,
left at home when she went out dancing.
She is the Dragonfly-Mother,

that cold
is only the rush of air

swiftness brings.
There is a summer
over the water, over

the river mirrors
where she hovers, a summer
fertile, abundant, where dreams
grow into acts and journeys.

Her children
are swimmers, nymphs and newts, metamorphic.
                              When she tells
her stories she listens; when she listens
she tells you the story you utter.

                              •

When I broke my promise,
and slept, and later
cooked and ate the food she had bought
and left in my kitchen,

I kept a tryst with myself,
a long promise that can be fulfilled
only poem by poem,
broken over and over.

          I too,
a creature, grow among reeds,
        in mud, in air,
in sunbright cold, in fever
of blue-gold zenith, winds
of passage.

        Dragonfly-Mother's
a messenger,
if I don't trust her
I can't keep faith.

        There is a summer
in the sleep
of broken promises, fertile dreams,
acts of passage, hovering
journeys over the fathomless waters.

Candles in Babylon

Through the midnight streets of Babylon
between the steel towers of their arsenals,
between the torture castles with no windows,
we race by barefoot, holding tight
our candles, trying to shield
the shivering flames, crying
'Sleepers Awake!'
                          hoping
the rhyme's promise was true,
that we may return
from this place of terror
home to a calm dawn and
the work we had just begun.

Williams: An Essay

His theme
over and over:

the twang of plucked
catgut
from which struggles
music,

the tufted swampgrass
quicksilvering
dank meadows,

a baby's resolute fury–metaphysic
of appetite and tension.

Not
the bald image, but always–
undulant, elusive, beyond reach
of any dull
staring eye–lodged

among the words, beneath
the skin of image: nerves,

muscles, rivers
of urgent blood, a mind

secret, disciplined, generous and
unfathomable.
                    Over

and over,
his theme
            hid itself and
smilingly reappeared.

                        He loved
persistence–but it must
be linked to invention: landing
backwards, 'facing
into the wind's teeth,'
                        to please him.

He loved
the lotus cup, fragrant
upon the swaying water, loved

the wily mud
pressing swart riches into its roots,

and the long stem of connection.

Mass for the Day of St. Thomas Didymus

i   Kyrie

O deep unknown, guttering candle,
beloved nugget lodged
in the obscure heart's
last recess,
have mercy upon us.

We choose from the past, tearing morsels to feed
pride or grievance.
We live in terror
of what we know:

death, death, and the world's
death we imagine
     and cannot imagine,
we who may be
the first and the last witness.

We live in terror
of what we do not know,
in terror of not knowing,
of the limitless, through which freefalling
forever, our dread
sinks and sinks,
         or
     of the violent closure of all.

Yet our hope lies
in the unknown,
in our unknowing.

O deep, remote unknown,
O deep unknown,
Have mercy upon us.

ii   Gloria

Praise the wet snow
        falling early.
Praise the shadow
        my neighbor's chimney casts on the tile roof
even this gray October day that should, they say,
have been golden.
                        Praise
the invisible sun burning beyond
    the white cold sky, giving us
light and the chimney's shadow.
Praise
god or the gods, the unknown,
that which imagined us, which stays
our hand,
our murderous hand,
                        and gives us
still,
in the shadow of death,
        our daily life,
        and the dream still
of goodwill, of peace on earth.
Praise
flow and change, night and
the pulse of day.

iii   Credo

I believe the earth
exists, and
in each minim mote
of its dust the holy
glow of thy candle.
Thou
unknown I know,
thou spirit,
giver,
lover of making, of the
wrought letter,
wrought flower,
iron, deed, dream.
Dust of the earth,
help thou my
unbelief. Drift,
gray become gold, in the beam of
vision. I believe and
interrupt my belief with
doubt. I doubt and
interrupt my doubt with belief. Be,
belovéd, threatened world.
            Each minim
mote.
            Not the poisonous
luminescence forced
out of its privacy,
the sacred lock of its cell
broken. No,
the ordinary glow
of common dust in ancient sunlight.
Be, that I may believe. Amen.

iv Sanctus

Powers and principalities–all the gods,
angels and demigods, eloquent animals, oracles,
storms of blessing and wrath–

>   all that Imagination
>   has wrought, has rendered,
>   striving, in throes of epiphany–

>   naming, forming–to give
>   to the Vast Loneliness
>   a hearth, a locus–

send forth their song towards
the harboring silence, uttering
the ecstasy of their names, the multiform
name of the Other, the known
Unknown, unknowable:

sanctus, hosanna, sanctus.

v Benedictus

Blesséd is that which comes in the name of the spirit,
that which bears
the spirit within it.

The name of the spirit is written
in woodgrain, windripple, crystal,

in crystals of snow, in petal, leaf,
moss and moon, fossil and feather,

blood, bone, song, silence,
very word of
very word,

flesh and
vision.

       (But what of the deft infliction
       upon the earth, upon the innocent,
       of hell by human hands?

       Is the word
       audible under or over the gross
       cacophony of malevolence?
       Yet to be felt
             on the palm, in the breast,
       by deafmute dreamers,
             a vibration
             known in the fibers of
             the tree of nerves, or witnessed
             by the third eye to which
             sight and sound are one?

       What of the emptiness,
       the destructive vortex that whirls
       no word with it?)

In the lion's indolence,
    there spirit is,
in the tiger's fierceness
    that does not provide in advance
but springs
         only as hunger prompts,
         and the hunger
         of its young.

Blessèd is that which utters
its being,
the stone of stone,
the straw of straw,
              for there
spirit is.
       But can the name

utter itself
        in the downspin of time?
Can it enter
        the void?
                      Blesséd
be the dust. From dust the world
utters itself. We have no other
hope, no knowledge.
        The word
chose to become
flesh. In the blur of flesh
we bow, baffled.

vi   Agnus Dei

Given that lambs
are infant sheep, that sheep
are afraid and foolish, and lack
the means of self-protection, having
neither rage nor claws,
venom nor cunning,
what then
is this 'Lamb of God'?

This pretty creature, vigorous
to nuzzle at milky dugs,
woolbearer, bleater,
leaper in air for delight of being, who finds in astonishment
four legs to land on, the grass
all it knows of the world?
        With whom we would like to play,
whom we'd lead with ribbons, but may not bring
into our houses because
it would soil the floor with its droppings?

What terror lies concealed
in strangest words, *O lamb
of God that taketh away*

135

the Sins of the World: an innocence
                        smelling of ignorance,
                        born in bloody snowdrifts,
                        licked by forebearing
dogs more intelligent than its entire flock put together?

                                    God then,
                    encompassing all things, is
                    defenseless? Omnipotence
                    has been tossed away, reduced
                    to a wisp of damp wool?

                                    And we,
                    frightened, bored, wanting
only to sleep till catastrophe
has raged, clashed, seethed and gone by without us,
                            wanting then
to awaken in quietude without remembrance of agony,

                        we who in shamefaced private hope
                        had looked to be plucked from fire and given
                        a bliss we deserved for having imagined it,

                            is it implied that *we*
                    must protect this perversely weak
                    animal, whose muzzle's nudgings
                    suppose there is milk to be found in us?
                    Must hold to our icy hearts
                    a shivering God?

                                •

So be it.
                Come, rag of pungent
                quiverings,
                            dim star.
                                    Let's try
                        if something human still

136

can shield you,
                    spark
of remote light.

Beginners

Dedicated to the memory of Karen Silkwood anal Eliot Gralla

'From too much love of living,
        Hope and desire set free,
Even the weariest river
            Winds somewhere to the sea–',

But we have only begun
to love the earth.

We have only begun
to imagine the fulness of life.

How could we tire of hope?
–so much is in bud.

How can desire fail?
–we have only begun

to imagine justice and mercy,
only begun to envision

how it might be
to live as siblings with beast and flower,
not as oppressors.

Surely our river
cannot already be hastening
into the sea of nonbeing?

Surely it cannot
drag, in the silt,
all that is innocent?
Not yet, not yet–
there is too much broken
that must be mended,

too much hurt we have done to each other
that cannot yet be forgiven.

We have only begun to know
the power that is in us if we would join
our solitudes in the communion of struggle.

So much is unfolding that must
complete its gesture,

so much is in bud.

Concurrence

Each day's terror, almost
a form of boredom–madmen
at the wheel and
stepping on the gas and
the brakes no good–
and each day one,
sometimes two, morning-glories,
faultless, blue, blue sometimes
flecked with magenta, each
lit from within with
the first sunlight.

138

Away he goes, the hour's delightful hero,
arrivederci: and his horse clatters
out of the courtyard, raising
a flurry of straw and scattering hens.

He turns in the saddle waving a plumed hat,
his saddlebags are filled with talismans,
mirrors, parchment histories, gifts and stones,
indecipherable clues to destiny.

He rides off in the dustcloud of his own
story, and when he has vanished she
who had stood firm to wave and watch
from the top step, goes in to the cool

flagstoned kitchen, clears honey and milk and bread
off the table, sweeps from the hearth
ashes of last night's fire, and climbs the stairs
to strip tumbled sheets from her wide bed.

                    Now the long-desired
visit is over. The heroine
is a scribe. Returned to solitude,
eagerly she re-enters the third room,

the room hung with tapestries, scenes that change
whenever she looks away. Here is her lectern,
here her writing desk. She picks a quill,
dips it, begins to write. But not of him.

Decipherings

for Guillevic

i

When I lose my center
of gravity
I can't fly:

levitation's
a stone
cast straight as a lark

to fall plumb
and rebound.

ii

Half a wheel's
a rising sun:
without spokes,
an arch:

half a loaf
reveals
the inner wheat:
leavened
transubstantiation.

iii

A child
grows in one's body,
pushes out and
breaks off:

                    nerves
denying their
non-existence
twist and pinch
long after:
after that otherness
floats
far,
thistledown engine,

up and
over
horizon's ramparts.

iv

Felt life
grows in one's mind:
each semblance

forms and
reforms cloudy
links with
the next

and the next:
chimes and
gamelan gongs

resound:

pondering,
picking the tesserae,
blue or
perhaps vermilion,

what one aches for
is the mosaic music
makes in one's ears

transformed.

The Avowal

For Carolyn Kizer and John Woodbridge,
Recalling Our Celebration
of the 300th Birthday of George Herbert, 1983

As swimmers dare
to lie face to the sky
and water bears them,
as hawks rest upon air
and air sustains them,
so would I learn to attain
freefall, and float
into Creator Spirit's deep embrace,
knowing no effort earns
that all-surrounding grace.

Delivered out of raw continual pain,
smell of darkness, groans of those others
to whom he was chained—

unchained, and led
past the sleepers,
door after door silently opening—
out!
    And along a long street's
majestic emptiness under the moon:

one hand on the angel's shoulder, one
feeling the air before him,
eyes open but fixed . . .

And not till he saw the angel had left him,
alone and free to resume
the ecstatic, dangerous, wearisome roads of
what he had still to do,
not till then did he recognize
this was no dream. More frightening
than arrest, than being chained to his warders:
he could hear his own footsteps suddenly.
Had the angel's feet
made any sound? He could not recall.
No one had missed him, no one was in pursuit.
He himself must be
the key, now, to the next door,
the next terrors of freedom and joy.

The Antiphon

*'L'Esprit souffle dans le silence
la où les mots n'ont plus de voix'*
Anon

And then once more
all is eloquent—rain,
raindrops on branches, pavement brick
humbly uneven, twigs of a storm-stripped hedge revealed
shining deep scarlet,
speckled whistler shabby and
unconcerned, anything—all
utters itself, blessedness
soaks the ground and its wintering seeds.

Of Being

I know this happiness
is provisional:

   the looming presences—
   great suffering, great fear—

   withdraw only
   into peripheral vision:

but ineluctable this shimmering
of wind in the blue leaves:

this flood of stillness
widening the lake of sky:

this need to dance,
this need to kneel:
    this mystery:

144

An awe so quiet
I don't know when it began.

A gratitude
had begun
to sing in me.

Was there
some moment
dividing
song from no song?

When does dewfall begin?

When does night
fold its arms over our hearts
to cherish them?

When is daybreak?

The Servant-Girl at Emmaus (A Painting by Velazquez)

She listens, listens, holding
her breath. Surely that voice
is his—the one
who had looked at her, once, across the crowd,
as no one ever had looked?
Had seen her? Had spoken as if to her?

Surely those hands were his,
taking the platter of bread from hers just now?
Hands he'd laid on the dying and made them well?

Surely that face—?

The man they'd crucified for sedition and blasphemy.
The man whose body disappeared from its tomb.
The man it was rumored now some women had seen this morning,
                                                          alive?

Those who had brought this stranger home to their table
don't recognize yet with whom they sit.
But she in the kitchen, absently touching
                        the winejug she's to take in,
a young Black servant intently listening,

swings round and sees
the light around him

                    'I learned that her name was Proverb.'

And the secret names
of all we meet who lead us deeper
into our labyrinth
of valleys and mountains, twisting valleys

146

and steeper mountains—
their hidden names are always,
like Proverb, promises:
Rune, Omen, Fable, Parable,
those we meet for only
one crucial moment, gaze to gaze,
or for years know and don't recognize

but of whom later a word
sings back to us
as if from high among leaves,
still near but beyond sight

drawing us from tree to tree
towards the time and the unknown place
where we shall know
what it is to arrive.

Hunting the Phoenix

Leaf through discolored manuscripts,
make sure no words
lie thirsting, bleeding,
waiting for rescue. No:
old loves half-
articulated, moments forced
out of the stream of perception
to play 'statue',
and never released—
they had no blood to shed.
You must seek
the ashy nest itself
if you hope to find
charred feathers, smouldering flightbones,
and a twist of singing flame
rekindling.

A wanderer comes at last
to the forest hut where it was promised
someone wise would receive him.
And there's no one there; birds and small animals
flutter and vanish, then return to observe.
No human eyes meet his.
But in the hut there's food,
set to keep warm beside glowing logs,
and fragrant garments to fit him, replacing
the rags of his journey,
and a bed of heather from the hills.
He stays there waiting. Each day the fire
is replenished, the pot refilled while he sleeps.
He draws up water from the well,
writes of his travels, listens for footsteps.
Little by little he finds
the absent sage is speaking to him,
is present.
                    This is the way
you have spoken to me, the way—startled—
I find I have heard you. When I need it,
a book or a slip of paper
appears in my hand, inscribed by yours: messages
waiting on cellar shelves, in forgotten boxes
until I would listen.
                    Your spirits relax;
now she is looking, you say to each other,
now she begins to see.

Caedmon

All others talked as if
talk were a dance.
Clodhopper I, with clumsy feet
would break the gliding ring.
Early I learned to
hunch myself
close by the door:
then when the talk began
I'd wipe my
mouth and wend
unnoticed back to the barn
to be with the warm beasts,
dumb among body sounds
of the simple ones.
I'd see by a twist
of lit rush the motes
of gold moving
from shadow to shadow
slow in the wake
of deep untroubled sighs.
The cows
munched or stirred or were still. I
was at home and lonely,
both in good measure. Until
the sudden angel affrighted me—light effacing
my feeble beam,
a forest of torches, feathers of flame, sparks upflying:
but the cows as before
were calm, and nothing was burning,
            nothing but I, as that hand of fire
touched my lips and scorched my tongue
and pulled my voice
                into the ring of the dance.

A voice from the dark called out,
        'The poets must give us
imagination of peace, to oust the intense, familiar
imagination of disaster. Peace, not only
the absence of war.'
                    But peace, like a poem,
is not there ahead of itself,
can't be imagined before it is made,
can't be known except
in the words of its making,
grammar of justice,
syntax of mutual aid.
                    A feeling towards it,
dimly sensing a rhythm, is all we have
until we begin to utter its metaphors,
learning them as we speak.
                        A line of peace might appear
if we restructured the sentence our lives are making,
revoked its reaffirmation of profit and power,
questioned our needs, allowed
long pauses . . .
                    A cadence of peace might balance its weight
on that different fulcrum; peace, a presence,
an energy field more intense than war,
might pulse then,
stanza by stanza into the world,
each act of living
one of its words, each word
a vibration of light—facets
of the forming crystal.

During a Son's Dangerous Illness

You could die before me—
I've known it
always, the
dreaded worst, 'unnatural' but
possible
in the play
of matter, matter and
growth and
fate.

                    •

My sister Philippa died
twelve years before I was born—
the perfect, laughing firstborn,
a gift to be cherished as my orphaned mother
had not been cherished. Suddenly:
death, a baby

cold and still.

                    •

Parent, child—death ignores
protocol, a sweep of its cape brushes
this one or that one at random
into the dust, it was
not even looking.
                    What becomes
of the past if the future
snaps off, brittle,
the present left as a jagged edge
opening on nothing?

                    •

Grief for the menaced world—lost rivers,
poisoned lakes—all creatures, perhaps,
to be fireblasted
                    off the
whirling cinder we
loved, but not enough . . .
The grief I'd know if I
lived into
your unthinkable death
is a splinter
of that selfsame grief,
infinitely smaller but
the same in kind:
one
stretching the mind's fibers to touch
eternal nothingness,
the other
tasting, in fear, the
desolation of
survival.

On a Theme from Julian's Chapter XX

Six hours outstretched in the sun, yes,
hot wood, the nails, blood trickling
into the eyes, yes—
but the thieves on their neighbor crosses
survived till after the soldiers
had come to fracture their legs, or longer.
Why single out this agony? What's
a mere six hours?
Torture then, torture now,
the same, the pain's the same,
immemorial branding iron,
electric prod.
Hasn't a child
dazed in the hospital ward they reserve
for the most abused, known worse?

This air we're breathing,
these very clouds, ephemeral billows
languid upon the sky's
moody ocean, we share
with women and men who've held out
days and weeks on the rack—
and in the ancient dust of the world
what particles
of the long tormented,
what ashes.

But Julian's lucid spirit leapt
to the difference:
perceived why no awe could measure
that brief day's endless length,
why among all the tortured
One only is 'King of Grief'.
The oneing, she saw, *the oneing
with the Godhead* opened Him utterly
to the pain of all minds, all bodies

—sands of the sea, of the desert—
from first beginning
to last day. The great wonder is
that the human cells of His flesh and bone
didn't explode
when utmost Imagination rose
in that flood of knowledge. Unique
in agony, Infinite strength, Incarnate,
empowered Him to endure
inside of history,
through those hours when He took to Himself
the sum total of anguish and drank
even the lees of that cup:

within the mesh of the web, Himself
woven within it, yet seeing it,
seeing it whole. *Every sorrow and desolation
He saw, and sorrowed in kinship.*

The Showings: Lady Julian of Norwich, 1342–1416

1

Julian, there are vast gaps we call black holes,
unable to picture what's both dense and vacant;

and there's the dizzying multiplication of all
language can name or fail to name, unutterable
swarming of molecules. All Pascal
imagined he could not stretch his mind to imagine
is known to exceed his dread.

And there's the earth of our daily history,
its memories, its present filled with the grain
of one particular scrap of carpentered wood we happen
to be next to, its waking light on one especial leaf,
this word or that, a tune in this key not another,
beat of our hearts *now,* good or bad,
dying or being born, eroded, vanishing—

And you ask us to turn our gaze
inside out, and see
a little thing, the size of a hazelnut, and believe
it is our world? Ask us to see it lying
in God's pierced palm? That it encompasses
every awareness our minds contain? All Time?
All limitless space given form in this
medieval enigma?
                    Yes, this is indeed
what you ask, sharing
the mystery you were shown: *all that is made:*
a little thing, the size of a hazelnut, held safe
in God's pierced palm.

2

What she petitioned for was never
instead of something else.
Thirty was older than it is now. She had not married
but was no starveling; if she had loved,
she had been loved. Death or some other destiny
bore him away, death or some other bride
changed him. Whatever that story,
long since she had travelled
through and beyond it. Somehow,
reading or read to, she'd spiralled
up within tall towers
of learning, steeples of discourse.
Bells in her spirit
rang new changes.
              Swept beyond event, one longing
outstripped all others: that reality,
supreme reality,
be witnessed. To desire wounds—
three, no less, no more—
is audacity, not, five centuries early, neurosis;
it's the desire to enact metaphor, for flesh to make known
to intellect (as uttered song
          makes known to voice,
          as image to eye)
make known in bone and breath
(and not die) God's agony.

'To understand her, you must imagine . . .'
A childhood, then;
the dairy's bowls of clabber, of rich cream,
ghost-white in shade, and outside
the midsummer gold, humming of dandelions.
To run back and forth, into the chill again,
the sweat of slate, a cake of butter
set on a green leaf—out once more
over slab of stone into hot light, hot
wood, the swinging gate!
A spire we think ancient split the blue
between two trees, a half-century old—
she thought it ancient.
Her father's hall, her mother's bower,
nothing was dull. The cuckoo
was changing its tune. In the church
there was glass in the windows, glass
colored like the world. You could see
Christ and his mother and his cross,
you could see his blood, and the throne of God.
In the fields
calves were lowing, the shepherd was taking the sheep
to new pasture.
                    Julian perhaps
not yet her name, this child's
that vivid woman.

4

God's wounded hand
reached out to place in hers
the entire world, 'round as a ball,
small as a hazelnut'. Just so one day
of infant light remembered
her mother might have given
into her two cupped palms
a newlaid egg, warm from the hen;
just so her brother
risked to her solemn joy
his delicate treasure,
a sparrow's egg from the hedgerow.
What can this be? *the eye of her understanding* marveled.

God for a moment in our history
placed in that five-fingered
human nest
the macrocosmic egg, sublime paradox,
brown hazelnut of All that Is—
made, and belov'd, and preserved.
As still, waking each day within
our microcosm, we find it, and ourselves.

Why did she laugh?
In scorn of malice.

What did they think?
They thought she was dying.

They caught her laugh?
Even the priest—

the dark small room
quivered with merriment,

all unaccountably
lightened.

If they had known
what she was seeing—

    the very
    spirit of evil,

    the Fiend they dreaded,
    seen to be oafish, ridiculous, vanquished—

what amazement! Stupid,
stupid his mar-plot malevolence!

Silly as his horns and
imaginary tail!

Why did her laughter
stop? Her mind moved on:

    the cost, the cost,
    the passion it took to undo

the deeds of malice.
The deathly

wounds and the anguished
heart.
And they?

They were abashed,
stranded in hilarity.

But when she recovered,
they told one another:

'Remember how we laughed
without knowing why?
That was the turning-point!'

6

Julian laughing aloud, glad
with *a most high inward happiness,*

Julian open calmly to dismissive judgements
flung backward down the centuries—
'delirium', 'hallucination';

Julian walking under-water
on the green hills of moss, the detailed sand and seaweed,
pilgrim of the depths, unfearing;

twenty years later carefully retelling
each unfading vision, each
pondered understanding;

Julian of whom we know
she had two serving-maids, Alice and Sara,
and kept a cat, and looked God in the face
and lived—

Julian nevertheless
said that *deeds are done so evil, injuries inflicted*
so great, it seems to us
impossible any good
can come of them—

any redemption, then, transform them . . .

She lived in dark times, as we do:
war, and the Black Death, hunger, strife,
torture, massacre. She knew
all of this, she felt it
sorrowfully, mournfully,
shaken as men shake
a cloth in the wind.

                  But Julian, Julian—
I turn to you:
                 you clung to joy though tears and sweat
rolled down your face like the blood
you watched pour down *in beads uncountable*
as rain from the eaves:
clung like an acrobat, by your teeth, fiercely,
to a cobweb-thin high-wire, your certainty
of infinite mercy, witnessed
with your own eyes, with outward sight
in your small room, with inward sight
in your untrammeled spirit—
knowledge we long to share:
Love was his meaning.

Variation and Reflection on a Theme by Rilke

(The Book of Hours, *Book I, Poem 7*)

1

If just for once the swing of cause and effect,
                         cause and effect,
would come to rest; if casual events would halt,
and the machine that supplies meaningless laughter
ran down, and my bustling senses, taking a deep breath
fell silent
and left my attention free at last . . .

then my thought, single and multifold,
could think you into itself
until it filled with you to the very brim,
bounding the whole flood of your boundlessness:

and at that timeless moment of possession,
fleeting as a smile, surrender you
and let you flow back into all creation.

2

There will never be that stillness.
Within the pulse of flesh,
in the dust of being, where we trudge,
      turning our hungry gaze this way and that,
the wings of the morning
brush through our blood
as cloud-shadows brush the land.
What we desire travels with us.
We must breathe time as fishes breathe water.
God's flight circles us.

161

Annunciation

'Hail, space for the uncontained God'
From the Agathistos Hymn,
Greece, VIc

We know the scene: the room, variously furnished,
almost always a lectern, a book; always
the tall lily.
    Arrived on solemn grandeur of great wings,
the angelic ambassador, standing or hovering,
whom she acknowledges, a guest.

But we are told of meek obedience. No one mentions
courage.
    The engendering Spirit
did not enter her without consent.
       God waited.

She was free
to accept or to refuse, choice
integral to humanness.

———————————

Aren't there annunciations
of one sort or another
in most lives?
    Some unwillingly
undertake great destinies,
enact them in sullen pride,
uncomprehending.
    More often
those moments
  when roads of light and storm
  open from darkness in a man or woman,
are turned away from

in dread, in a wave of weakness, in despair
and with relief.
Ordinary lives continue.
                    God does not smite them.
But the gates close, the pathway vanishes.

———————————————

She had been a child who played, ate, slept
like any other child—but unlike others,
wept only for pity, laughed
in joy not triumph.
Compassion and intelligence
fused in her, indivisible.

Called to a destiny more momentous
than any in all of Time,
she did not quail,
                    only asked
a simple, 'How can this be?'
and gravely, courteously,
took to heart the angel's reply,
perceiving instantly
the astounding ministry she was offered:

to bear in her womb
Infinite weight and lightness; to carry
in hidden, finite inwardness,
nine months of Eternity; to contain
in slender vase of being,
the sum of power—
in narrow flesh,
the sum of light.
                    Then bring to birth,
push out into air, a Man-child
needing, like any other,
milk and love—

but who was God.

163

This was the minute no one speaks of,
when she could still refuse.

A breath unbreathed,
                    Spirit,
                            suspended,
                                        waiting.

————————————

She did not cry, 'I cannot, I am not worthy,'
nor, 'I have not the strength.'
She did not submit with gritted teeth,
                                raging, coerced.
Bravest of all humans,
                    consent illumined her.
The room filled with its light,
the lily glowed in it,
                    and the iridescent wings.
Consent,
        courage unparalleled,
opened her utterly.

                                        The Braiding

The way the willow-bark
braids its furrows
is answered by the willow-branches
swaying their green leaf-weavings
over the river shallows,
assenting, affirming.

Lord, not you,
it is I who am absent.
At first
belief was a joy I kept in secret,
stealing alone
into sacred places:
a quick glance, and away—and back,
circling.
I have long since uttered your name
but now
I elude your presence.
I stop
to think about you, and my mind
at once
like a minnow darts away,
darts
into the shadows, into gleams that fret
unceasing over
the river's purling and passing.
Not for one second
will my self hold still, but wanders
anywhere,
everywhere it can turn. Not you,
it is I am absent.
You are the stream, the fish, the light,
the pulsing shadow,
you the unchanging presence, in whom all
moves and changes.
How can I focus my flickering, perceive
at the fountain's heart
the sapphire I know is there?

It is hard sometimes to drag ourselves
back to the love of morning
after we've lain in the dark crying out
O God, save us from the horror. . . .

God has saved the world one more day
even with its leaden burden of human evil;
we wake to birdsong.
And if sunlight's gossamer lifts in its net
the weight of all that is solid,
our hearts, too, are lifted,
swung like laughing infants;

but on gray mornings,
all incident—our own hunger,
the dear tasks of continuance,
the footsteps before us in the earth's
belovéd dust, leading the way—all,
is hard to love again
for we resent a summons
that disregards our sloth, and this
calls us, calls us.

The certainty of wings: a child's bold heart,
not, good little *Schul*-boy, Torah or Talmud
gave it to you, a practical vision:
wings were needed, why should people
plod forever on foot, not glide like herons
through the blue and white
promise unfolding
over their heads, over
the river's thawing?
Therefore the pedlar. (But why did they not
avail themselves of his wares?)

My father, as a child, sees the magic pedlar Marc Chagall was also to see a few years later. The one intuited that he carried wings, the other painted him, wingless but floating high over Vitepsk.

Later, *ochetz moy,* when you discovered
wings for your soul, the same bold heart
empowered you. From Prussia east and
    southward
verst after *verst* you willed the train to go
               faster,
skimming the rails home to the Dnieper valley.
You bore such news, so longed-for,
fulfilling a hope so ancient
it had almost become dry parchment,
            not hope any more.
At the station you hailed a *droshky,*
greeted the driver like a brother. At last
there was the street, there was the house:
but when you arrived
they would not listen.
They laughed at you. And then they wept.
But would not listen.

My father, as a student, discovers the Messiah,

and hurries home with the good news,

but is not believed.

St. Thomas Didymus

In the hot street at noon I saw him
                              a small man
              gray but vivid, standing forth
                                        beyond the crowd's buzzing
holding in desperate grip his shaking
                              teethgnashing son,

and thought him my brother.

I heard him cry out, weeping, and speak
                              those words,
Lord, I believe, help thou
                    mine unbelief,

and knew him
              my twin:

a man whose entire being
                    had knotted itself
into the one tightdrawn question,
                              Why,
why has this child lost his childhood in suffering,
                    why is this child who will soon be a man
tormented, torn, twisted?
                    Why is he cruelly punished
who has done nothing except be born?

The twin of my birth
                    was not so close
as that man I heard
              say what my heart
sighed with each beat, my breath silently
                                        cried in and out,
in and out.

168

After the healing,
                    he, with his wondering
newly peaceful boy, receded;
                            no one
dwells on the gratitude, the astonished joy,
                                    the swift
acceptance and forgetting.
                        I did not follow
to see their changed lives.
                        What I retained
was the flash of kinship.
                        Despite
all that I witnessed,
                    his question remained
my question, throbbed like a stealthy cancer,
                                    known
only to doctor and patient. To others
                            I seemed well enough.

So it was
            that after Golgotha
                            my spirit in secret
lurched in the same convulsed writhings
                                that tore that child
before he was healed.
                    And after the empty tomb
when they told me He lived, had spoken to Magdalen,
                                            told me
that though He had passed through the door like a ghost
                                    He had breathed on them
the breath of a living man—
                        even then
when hope tried with a flutter of wings
                                to lift me—
still, alone with myself,
                    my heavy cry was the same: *Lord,*
I believe,
            help thou mine unbelief.

I needed
        blood to tell me the truth,
the touch
        of blood. Even
my sight of the dark crust of it
                round the nailholes
didn't thrust its meaning all the way through
                  to that manifold knot in me
that willed to possess all knowledge,
                refusing to loosen
unless that insistence won
           the battle I fought with life.

But when my hand
          led by His hand's firm clasp
entered the unhealed wound,
             my fingers encountering
rib-bone and pulsing heat,
         what I felt was not
scalding pain, shame for my
          obstinate need,
but light, light streaming
        into me, over me, filling the room
as if I had lived till then
         in a cold cave, and now
coming forth for the first time,
          the knot that bound me unravelling,
I witnessed
        all things quicken to color, to form,
my question
        not answered but given
            its part
in a vast unfolding design lit
        by a risen sun.

The borderland—that's where, if one knew how,
one would establish residence. That watershed,
that spine, that looking-glass . . . I mean the edge
between impasto surface, burnt sienna, thick,
      striate, gleaming—swathes and windrows
      of carnal paint—
      or, canvas barely stained,
      where warp and weft peer through,

and fictive truth: a room, a vase, an open door
giving upon the clouds.

A step back, and you have
the likeness, its own world. Step to the wall again,
and you're so near the paint you could lick it,
you breathe its ghostly turpentine.
                          But there's an interface,
immeasurable, elusive—an equilibrium
just attainable, sometimes, when the attention's rightly poised,
where you are opulently received
by the bravura gestures hand and brush
proffer (as if a courtier twirled
a feathered velvet hat to bow you in)
and yet, without losing sight of one stroke,
              one scrape of the knife,
you are drawn through *into* that room, into
its air and temperature.

Couldn't one learn to maintain
that exquisite balance more than a second?
                   (One sees even
the pencilled understrokes, and shivers
in pleasure—*and* one's fingertips
touch the carpet's nubs of wool, the cold fruit in a bowl:
one almost sees
what lies beyond the window, past the frame, beyond . . .

171

Once, in dream,
                    the boat
pushed off from the shore.
You at the prow were the man—
all voice, though silent—who bound
rowers and voyagers to the needful journey,
the veiled distance, imperative mystery.

All the crouched effort,
            creak of oarlocks, odor of sweat,
            sound of waters
            running against us
was transcended: your gaze
held as we crossed. Its dragonfly blue
restored to us
                    a shimmering destination.

I had not read yet of your Nile journey,
the enabling voice
drawing that boat upstream in your parable.
Strange that I knew
your silence was just such a song.

A Traveler

If it's chariots or sandals,
I'll take sandals.
I like the high prow of the chariot,
the daredevil speed, the wind
a quick tune you can't
quite catch
            but I want to go
a long way

and I want to follow
paths where wheels deadlock.
                And I don't want always
to be among gear and horses,
        blood, foam, dust. I'd like
to wean myself from their strange allure.
I'll chance
the pilgrim sandals.

A Woodcut

(Jean Duvet, 1480–1561)

St. John, as Duvet's angel leads him
(roused from his arbor beyond
the river's moored boats and conversing swans)
through clouds, above the earthly orchards,
writes as he walks. But when he reaches
burnished Jerusalem, thronged with the blessèd,
most of them upward-gazing in adoration, some
leaning their arms on a balustrade
to dreamily scan implicit horizons
level with their celestial vantage-point,

he kneels wordless, gazing too—upward, outward,
back at the angel (now behind him), downward, inward—
his ink-bottle slung at his hip
as before, but his notebook
vanished, perhaps discarded.

Intricate and untraceable
weaving and interweaving,
dark strand with light:

designed, beyond
all spiderly contrivance,
to link, not to entrap:

elation, grief, joy, contrition, entwined;
shaking, changing,
                    forever
                            forming,
                                    transforming:

all praise,
        all praise to the
                    great web.

Ikon: The Harrowing of Hell

Down through the tomb's inward arch
He has shouldered out into Limbo
to gather them, dazed, from dreamless slumber:
the merciful dead, the prophets,
the innocents just His own age and those
unnumbered others waiting here
unaware, in an endless void He is ending
now, stooping to tug at their hands,
to pull them from their sarcophagi,
dazzled, almost unwilling. Didmas,
neighbor in death, Golgotha dust
still streaked on the dried sweat of his body

174

no one had washed and anointed, is here,
for sequence is not known in Limbo;
the promise, given from cross to cross
at noon, arches beyond sunset and dawn.
All these He will swiftly lead
to the Paradise road: they are safe.
That done, there must take place that struggle
no human presumes to picture:
living, dying, descending to rescue the just
from shadow, were lesser travails
than this: to break
through earth and stone of the faithless world
back to the cold sepulchre, tearstained
stifling shroud; to break from *them*
back into breath and heartbeat, and walk
the world again, closed into days and weeks again,
wounds of His anguish open, and Spirit
streaming through every cell of flesh
so that if mortal sight could bear
to perceive it, it would be seen
His mortal flesh was lit from within, now,
and aching for home. He must return,
first, in Divine patience, and know
hunger again, and give
to humble friends the joy
of giving Him food—fish and a honeycomb.

Lent 1988

175

Suspended

I had grasped God's garment in the void
but my hand slipped
on the rich silk of it.
The 'everlasting arms' my sister loved to remember
must have upheld my leaden weight
from falling, even so,
for though I claw at empty air and feel
nothing, no embrace,
I have not plummetted.

Settling

I was welcomed here—clear gold
of late summer, of opening autumn,
the dawn eagle sunning himself on the highest tree,
the mountain revealing herself unclouded, her snow
tinted apricot as she looked west,
tolerant, in her steadfastness, of the restless sun
forever rising and setting.
                              Now I am given
a taste of the grey foretold by all and sundry,
a grey both heavy and chill. I've boasted I would not care,
I'm London-born. And I won't. I'll dig in,
into my days, having come here to live, not to visit.
Grey is the price
of neighboring with eagles, of knowing
a mountain's vast presence, seen or unseen.

Elusive

The mountain comes and goes
on the horizon,

      a rhythm elusive as that of a sea-wave
      higher than all the rest, riding to shore
      flying its silver banners—

you count to seven, but no,
its measure
      slips by you with each recurrence.

Effacement

Today the mountain
is cloud,
pale cone of shadow
veiled by a paler scrim—

majestic presence become
one cloud among others,
humble vapor,
barely discernible,

like the archangel walking
with Tobias on dusty roads.

Presence

Though the mountain's the same warm-tinted ivory
as the clouds (as if a red ground had been laid beneath
not quite translucent white) and though the clouds
disguise its shoulders, and rise tall to left and right,
and soften the pale summit with mist,

                                    yet one perceives
the massive presence, obdurate, unconcerned
among those filmy guardians.

Open Secret

Perhaps one day I shall let myself
approach the mountain—
hear the streams which must flow down it,
lie in a flowering meadow, even
touch my hand to the snow.
Perhaps not. I have no longing to do so.
I have visited other mountain heights.
This one is not, I think, to be known
by close scrutiny, by touch of foot or hand
or entire outstretched body; not by any
familiarity of behavior, any acquaintance
with its geology or the scarring roads
humans have carved in its flanks.
This mountain's power
lies in the open secret of its remote
apparition, silvery low-relief
coming and going moonlike at the horizon,
always loftier, lonelier, than I ever remember.

You danced ahead of me, I took
none of those last steps with you
when your *enchainement* led you
uphill to the hospital and a death sentence
or before that when language
twirled round and tripped your voice.
Dancers must learn to walk
slowly across a stage, unfaltering;
we practiced that, long ago.
You faltered, but only in the wings,
that week when *timor mortis*
lunged at you. And you shook off
that devouring terror, held up
your head, straightened
your back, and moved in grace
(they tell me—I was not at your side
but far away,
intent on a different music)
into the light of that last stage,
a hospice garden, where you could say,
breathing the ripened fragrance of August mornings,
'yes, and evenings too are beautiful.'

Flowers of Sophia

Flax, chicory, scabious—
flowers with ugly names,
they grow in waste ground, sidewalk edges,
fumes, grime, trash.
Each kind has a delicate form, distinctive;
it would be pleasant to draw them.
All are a dreamy blue,
a gentle mysterious blue,
wise beyond comprehension.

179

An old man sleeping in the evening train,
face upturned, mouth discreetly closed,
hands clasped, with fingers interlaced.
Those large hands
lie on the fur lining of his wife's coat
he's holding for her, and the fur
looks like a limp dog, docile and affectionate.
The man himself is a peasant
in city clothes, moderately prosperous—
rich by the standards of his youth;
one can read that in his hands,
his sleeping features.
How tired he is, how tired.
I called him old, but then I remember
my own age, and acknowledge he's likely
no older than I. But in the dimension
that moves with us but itself keeps still
like the bubble in a carpenter's level,
I'm fourteen, watching the faces I saw each day
on the train going in to London,
and never spoke to; or guessing
from a row of shoes what sort of faces
I'd see if I raised my eyes.
Everyone has an unchanging age (or sometimes two)
carried within them, beyond expression.
This man perhaps
is ten, putting in a few hours most days
in a crowded schoolroom, and a lot more
at work in the fields; a boy who's always
making plans to go fishing his first free day.
The train moves through the dark quite swiftly
(the Italian dark, as it happens)
with its load of people, each
with a conscious destination, each
with a known age and that other,

the hidden one—except for those
still young, or not young but slower to focus,
who haven't reached yet that state of being
which will become
not a point of arrest but a core
around which the mind develops, reflections circle,
events accrue—a center.
                              A girl with braids
sits in this corner seat, invisible,
pleased with her solitude. And across from her
an invisible boy, dreaming. She knows
she cannot imagine his dreams. Quite swiftly
we move through our lives; swiftly, steadily the train
rocks and bounces onward through sleeping fields,
our unknown stillness
holding level as water sealed in glass.

Witness

Sometimes the mountain
is hidden from me in veils
of cloud, sometimes
I am hidden from the mountain
in veils of inattention, apathy, fatigue,
when I forget or refuse to go
down to the shore or a few yards
up the road, on a clear day,
to reconfirm
that witnessing presence.

Maybe He looked indeed
much as Rembrandt envisioned Him
in those small heads that seem in fact
portraits of more than a model.
A dark, still young, very intelligent face,
a soul-mirror gaze of deep understanding, unjudging.
That face, in extremis, would have clenched its teeth
in a grimace not shown in even the great crucifixions.
The burden of humanness (I begin to see) exacted from Him
that He taste also the humiliation of dread,
cold sweat of wanting to let the whole thing go,
like any mortal hero out of his depth,
like anyone who has taken a step too far
and wants herself back.
The painters, even the greatest, don't show how,
in the midnight Garden,
or staggering uphill under the weight of the Cross,
He went through with even the human longing
to simply cease, to not be.
Not torture of body,
not the hideous betrayals humans commit
nor the faithless weakness of friends, and surely
not the anticipation of death (not then, in agony's grip)
was Incarnation's heaviest weight,
but this sickened desire to renege,
to step back from what He, Who was God,
had promised Himself, and had entered
time and flesh to enact.
Sublime acceptance, to be absolute, had to have welled
up from those depths where purpose
drifted for mortal moments.

What Harbinger?

Glitter of grey
oarstrokes over
the waveless, dark,
secretive water.
A boat is moving
toward me
slowly, but who
is rowing and what
it brings I can't
yet see.

Le Motif

Southwest the moon
full and clear,

eastward, the sky
reddening, cloudless
over fir trees, the dark hill.

I remember, decades ago,
'day coming and the moon not gone,'
the low ridge of the Luberon
beyond the well

and Ste. Victoire
shifting its planes and angles
yet again.

A sunset of such aqueous hints, subdued
opaline gleamings, so much grey among its
wan folds, fading
tangerine roses;

> and in a rosetree—not a rosetree,
> a young tree of some other species
> which has become the noble
> support, patient, perhaps eager,
> of a capricious Gloire de Dijon—

in this green
symbiosis of elder and wildening
rose, the evening wind is pulsing,
and the sound nearby
of a saxophone, slowly wistful
without being strictly sad.

For the first time, the certainty of return
to this imprinted scene, unchanging but for the height
of green thicket, rising year by year
beyond the cobwebbed windowpanes,
can not be assumed.

The Mystery of Deep Candor

Intervals
so frank,
open and major as you like,
rhythms
a child could keep—

only Haydn dared
make magic from such
morning suns,
roadside gold, each dandelion
dipped in his elixir,
the secret depths of candor.

Sojourns in the Parallel World

We live our lives of human passions,
cruelties, dreams, concepts,
crimes and the exercise of virtue
in and beside a world devoid
of our preoccupations, free
from apprehension—though affected,
certainly, by our actions. A world
parallel to our own though overlapping.
We call it 'Nature;' only reluctantly
admitting ourselves to be 'Nature' too.
Whenever we lose track of our own obsessions,
our self-concerns, because we drift for a minute,
an hour even, of pure (almost pure)
response to that insouciant life:
cloud, bird, fox, the flow of light, the dancing
pilgrimage of water, vast stillness
of spellbound ephemerae on a lit windowpane,
animal voices, mineral hum, wind
conversing with rain, ocean with rock, stuttering
of fire to coal—then something tethered
in us, hobbled like a donkey on its patch
of gnawed grass and thistles, breaks free.
No one discovers
just where we've been, when we're caught up again
into our own sphere (where we must
return, indeed, to evolve our destinies)
—but we have changed, a little.

For years the dead
were the terrible weight of their absence,
the weight of what one had not put in their hands.
Rarely a visitation—dream or vision—
lifted that load for a moment, like someone
standing behind one and briefly taking
the heft of a frameless pack.
But the straps remained, and the ache—
though you can learn not to feel it
except when malicious memory
pulls downward with sudden force.
Slowly there comes a sense
that for some time the burden
has been what you need anyway.
How flimsy to be without it, ungrounded, blown
hither and thither, colliding with stern solids.
And then they begin to return, the dead:
but not as visions. They're not
separate now, not to be seen, no,
it's they who see: they displace,
for seconds, for minutes, maybe longer,
the mourner's gaze with their own. Just now,
that shift of light, arpeggio
on ocean's harp—
not the accustomed bearer
of heavy absence saw it, it was perceived
by the long-dead, long absent, looking
out from within one's wideopen eyes.

For Those Whom the Gods Love Less

When you discover
your new work travels the ground you had traversed
decades ago, you wonder, panicked,
'Have I outlived my vocation? Said already
all that was mine to say?'
                              There's a remedy—
only one—for the paralysis seizing your throat to mute you,
numbing your hands: Remember the great ones, remember
     Cezanne
doggedly *sur le motif,* his mountain
a tireless noonday angel he grappled like Jacob,
demanding reluctant blessing. Remember James rehearsing
over and over his theme, the loss
of innocence and the attainment
(note by separate note sounding its tone
until by accretion a chord resounds) of somber
understanding. Each life in art
goes forth to meet dragons that rise from their bloody scales
in cyclic rhythm: Know and forget, know and forget.
It's not only
the passion for *getting it right* (though it's that, too)
it's the way
radiant epiphanies recur, recur,
consuming, pristine, unrecognized—
until remembrance dismays you. And then, look,
some inflection of light, some wing of shadow
is other, unvoiced. You can, you must
proceed.

Conversion of Brother Lawrence

'Let us enter into
ourselves, Time
presses.'
Brother Lawrence
1611–1691

1

What leafless tree plunging
into what pent sky was it
convinced you Spring, bound to return
in all its unlikelihood, was a word
of God, a Divine message?
Custom, natural reason, are everyone's assurance;
we take the daylight for granted, the moon,
the measured tides. A particular tree, though,
one day in your eighteenth winter,
said more, an oracle. Clumsy footman,
apt to drop the ornate objects handed to you,
cursed and cuffed by butlers and grooms,
your inner life unsuspected,
you heard, that day, a more-than-green
voice from the stripped branches.
Wooden lace, a celestial geometry, uttered
more than familiar rhythms of growth.
It said *By the Grace of God.*
Midsummer rustled around you that wintry moment.
Was it elm, ash, poplar, a fruit-tree, your rooted
twig-winged angel of annunciation?

2

Out from the chateau park it sent you
(by some back lane, no doubt,
not through the wide gates of curled iron),

by ways untold, by soldier's marches, to the obscure
clatter and heat of a monastery kitchen,
a broom's rhythmic whisper for music,
your torment the drudgery of household ledgers. Destiny
without visible glory. 'Time pressed.' Among pots and pans,
heart-still through the bustle of chores,
your labors, hard as the pain in your lame leg,
grew slowly easier over the years, the years
when, though your soul felt darkened, heavy, worthless,
yet God, you discovered, never abandoned you but walked
at your side keeping pace as comrades had
on the long hard roads of war. You entered then
the unending 'silent secret conversation',
the life of steadfast attention.
Not work transformed you; work, even drudgery,
was transformed: that discourse
pierced through its monotones, infused them
with streams of sparkling color.
What needed doing, you did; journeyed if need be
on rocking boats, lame though you were,
to the vineyard country to purchase the year's wine
for a hundred Brothers, laughably rolling yourself
over the deck-stacked barrels when you couldn't
keep your footing; and managed deals with the vintners
to your own surprise, though business was nothing to you.
Your secret was not the craftsman's delight in process,
which doesn't distinguish work from pleasure—
your way was not to exalt nor avoid
the Adamic legacy, you simply made it irrelevant:
everything faded, thinned to nothing, beside
the light which bathed and warmed, the Presence
your being had opened to. Where it shone,

there life was, and abundantly; it touched
your dullest task, and the task was easy.
                    Joyful, absorbed,
you 'practiced the presence of God' as a musician
practices hour after hour his art:
'A stone before the carver,'
you 'entered into yourself.'

Pentimento

To be discerned
                    only by those
                                        alert to likelihood—

the mountain's form
                    beneath the milky radiance
                                        which revokes it.

It lingers—
            a draft
                    the artist may return to.

The golden particles
descend, descend,
traverse the water's
depth and come to rest
on the level bed
of the well until,
the full descent
accomplished, water's
absolute transparence
is complete, unclouded
by constellations
of bright sand.
Is this
the place where you
are brought in meditation?
Transparency
seen for itself—
as if its quality
were not, after all,
to enable
perception *not* of itself?
With a wand
of willow I again
trouble the envisioned pool,
the cloudy nebulae
form and disperse,
the separate
grains again
slowly, slowly
perform their descent,
and again
stillness ensues,

and the mystery
of that sheer
clarity, is it water indeed,
or air, or light?

Primary Wonder

Days pass when I forget the mystery.
Problems insoluble and problems offering
their own ignored solutions
jostle for my attention, they crowd its antechamber
along with a host of diversions, my courtiers, wearing
their colored clothes; cap and bells.
                                        And then
once more the quiet mystery
is present to me, the throng's clamor
recedes: the mystery
that there is anything, anything at all,
let alone cosmos, joy, memory, everything,
rather than void: and that, O Lord,
Creator, Hallowed One, You still,
hour by hour sustain it.

The crows are tossing themselves
recklessly in the random winds
of spring.
        One friend has died, one disappeared
      (for now, at least) leaving no address;
      I've lost the whereabouts
      of a wandering third. That seems to be,
      this year, the nature of this season.
      Is it a message about relinquishment?
Across the water, rain's veil, gray silk,
flattens the woods to two dimensions.
While close at hand
the crows' black fountain
jets and falls, jets and blows
this way and that.
How they scoop themselves
up from airy nadirs!

'In Whom We Live and Move and Have Our Being'

Birds afloat in air's current,
sacred breath? No, not breath of God,
it seems, but God
the air enveloping the whole
globe of being.
It's we who breathe, in, out, in, the sacred,
leaves astir, our wings
rising, ruffled—but only the saints
take flight. We cower
in cliff-crevice or edge out gingerly
on branches close to the nest. The wind
marks the passage of holy ones riding
that ocean of air. Slowly their wake
reaches us, rocks us.
But storm or still,
numb or poised in attention,
we inhale, exhale, inhale,
encompassed, encompassed.

Celebration

Brilliant, this day—a young virtuoso of a day.
Morning shadows cut by sharpest scissors,
deft hands. And every prodigy of green—
whether it's ferns or lichen or needles
or impatient points of bud on spindly bushes—

greener than ever before.
                              And the way the conifers
hold new cones to the light for blessing,
a festive rite, and sing the oceanic chant the wind
transcribes for them!
A day that shines in the cold
like a first-prize brass band swinging along the street
of a coal-dusty village, wholly at odds
with the claims of reasonable gloom.

First Love

It was a flower.

There had been,
before I could even speak,
another infant, girl or boy unknown,
who drew me—I had
an obscure desire to become
connected in some way to this other,
even to *be* what I faltered after, falling
to hands and knees, crawling
a foot or two, clambering
up to follow further until
arms swooped down to bear me away.
But that one left no face, had exchanged
no gaze with me.

This flower:
                  suddenly
there was *Before I saw it,* the vague
past, and *Now.* Forever. Nearby

was the sandy sweep of the Roman Road,
and where we sat the grass
was thin. From a bare patch
of that poor soil, solitary,
sprang the flower, face upturned,
looking completely, openly
into my eyes.
   I was barely
old enough to ask and repeat its name.

'Convolvulus,' said my mother.
Pale shell-pink, a chalice
no wider across than a silver sixpence.

It looked at me, I looked
back, delight
filled me as if
I, not the flower,
were a flower and were brimful of rain.
And there was endlessness.
Perhaps through a lifetime what I've desired
has always been to return
to that endless giving and receiving, the wholeness
of that attention,
that once-in-a-lifetime
secret communion.

Before the Wholesale Produce Market
moved to the Bronx, what wild
Arabian scenes there'd be each night
across from our 5th floor window—
the trucks arriving from all over
as if at a caravanserai under the weird
orange-bright streetlights
(or was it the canvas awnings that were orange,
sheltering the carrots, the actual oranges . . .)
Great mounds of fruit, mountain ranges
of vegetables spread in the stalls, and now
more unloading, and the retail trucks
rolling up to bargain and buy till dawn . . .
Unemployed men, casual labor, hung around,
waiting for clean-up jobs; some were glad
to get some bruised produce if no work.
And the Catholic Worker pickup
came by at the last
for anything unsold, unsaleable (but not
uncookable). In the '60s
there was the Bowery, yes, and ordinary
urban winos, but not
throngs of homeless men
and hardly ever a homeless woman except
for those you'd see down at Maryhouse or sometimes
(conspicuous, embarrassing), in the waiting room at Grand Central.
There were men, though, among those frequenting the market,
who clearly had no fixed abode; we thought of them
as old fashioned hobos.
Some time in the night, or weekends
when the big parking lot, the whole
commercial neighborhood (vanished now), was deserted,
they'd build fires in old metal barrels
and sit round them on upturned crates
roasting fallen potatoes they'd salvaged,

(a regular feast once when a truck
lost its load) and talking, telling stories,
passing a bottle if they had one.
The war was (remotely) gearing up,
Vietnam a still unfamiliar name,
the men were down on their luck,
some White, some Black, not noticeably hostile,
most of them probably drunks:
you couldn't call it
a Golden Age; and yet
around those fires, those roasting potatoes,
you could see, even from our top-storey windows,
not even down there catching the smoky
potato-skin smell or hearing
fragments of talk and laughter—*something*
—you name it, if you know, I can't . . .
something you might call blessèd? Is that hyperbole? Something kind?
Something not to be found in the '90s, anyway.
Something it seems we'll have to enter the next millennium
lacking, and for the young,
                              unknown to memory.

The mountain's daily speech is silence

The mountain's daily speech is silence.
Profound as the Great Silence
between the last Office and the first.
Uninterrupted as the silence God maintains
throughout the layered centuries.
All the mountain's moods,
frank or evasive,
its whiteness, its blueness,
are shown to sight alone.
Yet it is known
that fire seethes in its depths
and will surely rise one day, breaking open
the mute imperturbable summit. Will the roar of eruption be
the mountain's own repressed voice,
or that of the fire? Does the mountain
harbor a demon distinct from itself?

Once Only

All which, because it was
flame and song and granted us
joy, we thought we'd do, be, revisit,
turns out to have been what it was
that *once*, only; every initiation
did not begin
a series, a build-up: the marvelous
      did happen in our lives, our stories
      are not drab with its absence: but don't
expect now to return for more. Whatever more

there will be will be
unique as those were unique. Try
to acknowledge the next
song in its body-halo of flames as utterly
present, as now or never.

The Métier of Blossoming

Fully occupied with growing—that's
the amaryllis. Growing especially
at night: it would take
only a bit more patience than I've got
to sit keeping watch with it till daylight;
the naked eye could register every hour's
increase in height. Like a child against a barn door,
proudly topping each year's achievement,
steadily up
goes each green stem, smooth, matte,
traces of reddish purple at the base, and almost
imperceptible vertical ridges
running the length of them:
Two robust stems from each bulb,
sometimes with sturdy leaves for company,
elegant sweeps of blade with rounded points.
Aloft, the gravid buds, shiny with fullness.
One morning—and so soon!—the first flower
has opened when you wake. Or you catch it poised
in a single, brief
moment of hesitation.
Next day, another,

shy at first like a foal,
even a third, a fourth,
carried triumphantly at the summit
of those strong columns, and each
a Juno, calm in brilliance,
a maiden giantess in modest splendor.
If humans could be
that intensely whole, undistracted, unhurried,
swift from sheer
unswerving impetus! If we could blossom
out of ourselves, giving
nothing imperfect, withholding nothing!

It was the way
as they climbed the steps
they appeared bit by bit
yet swiftly—
the tops of their hats
then their faces
looking in as they reached
the top step by the door, then
as I flung the door open
their dear corporeal selves,
first him, then her. It was
the simultaneously
swift and gradual advent
of such mercy after
I had been wounded.
It was the little familiar
net attached to her hat,
it was especially
the thick soft cloth of his black
clerical overcoat,
and their short stature
and their complete
comforting embrace,
the long-dead
visiting time from eternity.

*"I've always written rather directly about my life,
my concerns at any particular time."*

Denise Levertov's life (1923–1997) spans nearly three quarters of the most violent century in recorded history. She lived through the aftermath of the First World War, the world-wide Depression, the rise of the mass movements of fascism and communism, the Second World War, the Atomic Age, neocolonialism, the Korean, Vietnam and Gulf Wars, as well as countless smaller and regional wars. The framework of the peace, anti-nuclear and ecology movements, within which she lived her private and inner life appears as background and sometimes foreground in her poetry. All her life, she wrote out of her family: as daughter of older parents, as younger sister, later as wife and mother. She wrote as friend and lover, as social activist. She wrote from her life as outsider, pilgrim and wanderer, as a transplant never fully at home, as an "airplant" rather than a rooted one.

> Among Jews a Goy, among Gentiles (secular or Christian) a Jew or at least half Jew (which was good or bad according to their degree of anti-semitism), among Anglo-Saxons a Celt, in Wales a Londoner who not only did not speak Welsh, but was not imbued with Welsh attitudes; among school children a strange exception whom they did not know whether to envy or mistrust—all of these anomalies predicted my later experience: I so often feel English, or perhaps European, in the United States, while in England I sometimes feel American …[1]

She was born in Ilford, Essex, near London, to a Welsh Congregationalist mother and a father who was Russian, a Hasidic Jew who had become a Christian and an Anglican priest. She and Olga, nine years her elder, were educated at home, in an atmosphere both intensely intellectual and deeply spiritual, at once cosmopolitan and tightly inward and enclosed. Both parents were scholarly. Her father wrote extensively on Jewish mysticism and the connections between Judaism and Christianity. He was a passionate, eloquent preacher. Both girls were intellectually precocious and encouraged to be old beyond their years. The parents entertained serious scholars, theologians and artists, and welcomed many refugees from Naziism into their home, and the girls were always drawn into that company. When she was twelve, Denise Levertov sent some of her poems to T. S. Eliot, then serving on a church commission with Paul Levertoff, who sent her encouragement and criticism as to an adult. The home was a place of intense intellectual activity and conversation, but also one of long, deep silences and solitude.

Their mother's approach to education was unorthodox. While the arts, history, languages, mythology, fairy-tales, novels, poetry, and imaginative writing of all kinds were highly favored, she was not interested in science and apparently considered mathematics simply unimportant, so even basic arithmetic came hard for Denise Levertov all her life. Her mother's teaching and the family atmosphere made her a lifelong autodidact, gifted in languages, the arts, music, the literature of many cultures, and natural history. She has called it an ideal pedagogy for her but very bad for her sister. Her formal education ended when she was twelve, when she began to study ballet, largely at Olga's insistence. At the outbreak of the Second World War she served briefly in the Land Army, where, for a time, she was assigned to a turkey farm. In 1984, she recalled how terrified she was to approach the fence at feeding time and have thousands of madly shrieking turkeys rush at her. In panic, she would hurl handfuls of feed at them. "I practically *stoned* them!" She shifted to nursing and qualified as a practical nurse. She was steadily writing poetry and had her first poem, "Listening to Distant Guns," published in 1940, when she was seventeen. In 1946, the prestigious Cresset Press, edited by John Hayward, published her first book, *The Double Image.* The publisher introduced the book thus:

> ... Miss Levertoff examines and expounds with delicate sensibility and understanding the personal dilemma of many of her contemporaries,... the conflict, in heart as well as mind, be-

tween frustration and disenchantment, on the one hand, and resolve and conviction on the other. While her mood is unmistakably that of her generation, her expression of it is as certainly her own.

After the war, she traveled on the continent and worked as a nurse in Paris, where she met Mitchell Goodman, an American pursuing free-lance study under the G.I. Bill. They married in 1947, moved to the United States in 1948, where their only child, Nikolai, was born in 1949. For the next several years, the family lived in New York, in France, in Mexico, and again in New York. Mitchell Goodman supported the family with free-lance travel writing. In 1949, Denise Levertov's poetry was included in Kenneth Rexroth's *New British Poets*, where she was identified as a representative of British New Romanticism; and after her poems appeared in the influential American publications *Origin* and *Black Mountain Review*, leading critics with a penchant for easy labels called her a "Black Mountain poet," though she had never set foot on that campus nor been otherwise involved. She was becoming an American rather than an English poet. "… I think that I was able to become American because I wasn't really anything. I was many things and no one thing."[2] Certainly her developing friendships with Robert Creeley, Robert Duncan, and above all with William Carlos Williams profoundly influenced that transformation. She first became acquainted with the writings of Williams and Wallace Stevens while she was living in Paris, shortly before coming to the United States. "We bought *In the American Grain* and the *Selected Poems*, and I had an *immediate* feeling that here was something, something that was going to speak to me." At first, she could not tell how the poems would sound. "I didn't understand the rhythmic structure, and often I didn't understand the … specifically American references," but after living in the United States for a while, "my ear had gotten used to certain cadences," and to the pace of life, and the movement of the day, which she found different from those of Europe. Of the influence of Williams and Stevens on her poetry, she said in 1965:

[Williams] gave me the use of the American language. He showed me how it and the American idiom could be used; and more than that, he gave me instance after instance of how one's most ordinary experience could be shown in the poems as it was, invested with wonder. From Stevens … I think I've gotten, over and over again, a sense of magic, the same almost surrealist magic that Garcia Lorca has—a reminder of how, at a certain pitch of awareness of language, one can make marvelous leaps. Stevens distorts my senses, like Rimbaud, you know."[3]

Male writers have *mentors* from whom they learn and with whom they become colleagues; women writers with the same kind of relationship with an older writer are apt to be labeled the "*disciple* of …." Levertov is frequently glibly pigeonholed as a "disciple of Williams" in the same way she is attached to "the Black Mountain School," but as the recent publication of the Williams-Levertov letters demonstrates, they learned from each other. Levertov knew herself indebted to Williams for teaching her the American idiom, and he was indebted to her, at a low point in his life, for a subtle, sophisticated and affirmative understanding of his work. She is one of his most perceptive readers and interpreters. She explicates his dictum "no ideas but in things" (a phrase which he shares with Wallace Stevens) so as to unite idea and thing, the concrete details from which larger perceptions emerge. Her poem "Williams: an Essay" celebrates what he loved, persistence linked to invention and the long stem of connection, and her essays document his craft as a stepping-stone of the imagination toward her own mature practice.

Williams, then, was a profound and enduring influence on Levertov's poetic craft, but, voracious reader and autodidact that she was, she learned from many sources, among them writers as various as Kenneth Rexroth, Robert Creeley, Herbert Read, H.D., Rainer Maria Rilke. The forthcoming edition of letters between Levertov and Robert Duncan will show another example of intense mutual influence. Before Williams, she knew intimately the poetry and the poetic practice of the Romantics, Wordsworth, Coleridge, Shelley, Blake and Keats. She quoted Keats's letters frequently, and a book she bought, read and annotated in 1942 was *Anima Poetae,* the first published selections from Coleridge's notebooks. As early as 1942 she had begun to read Rilke's letters, then his poetry. These writers are presences and touchstones in her poetry throughout her life. She was also deeply read in the Victorian novelists, essayists and poets.

Levertov is an especially good test case of what we might mean when we talk of "influences." She reads widely and deeply, remembers, and uses what she reads. Key phrases from Keats, Rilke, Swinburne serve as shorthand for what she wants to say or touchstones for moods and apperceptions, but the touchstone phrases may not have the same invariant meaning for her in different contexts. In some poems we find direct quotations from other writers, but that does not necessarily mean a deeper "flowing-in" of themes, ideas, or ways of conceiving of poems into her work. Swinburne's lines from "The Garden of Proserpine," "from too much love of living…"— which she always consciously misquotes because that is how she recalls them—frequently serve as an index of her feelings, but she never becomes Swinburnian. We may hear echoes of another writer, sometimes as a kind of reply to him or her. For example, "Another Journey" takes its start from Stevens' "Farewell to Florida" and "Broken Glass" owes something to Williams' "Spring and All." In her later work, Levertov does not create translations but "variations on a theme," and in one case a variation and commentary on a theme by Rilke. After she moves to Seattle, she becomes invested in both the landscape of the Northwest, the ecological consciousness of its writers, and "the strong influence of Chinese and Japanese poetry and of Buddhism on a people dwelling in a landscape which … often seems to resemble one of those great scroll paintings of Asian art…." But Levertov's imagination is profoundly assimilative, not imitative. She takes her sources of inspiration deep into her consciousness, lets them make their own connections with one another, then come into her conscious life transformed, made into something which is her own. Not merely phrases or tricks of others' craft but their ways of seeing, depth of vision, and intensity of vocation get drawn into her life, even into her dreams, and become living streams which enter, mingle with, and become absorbed into the river of her own thinking-feeling. This is another way to say that what Levertov reads becomes part of what happens to her, part of the life about which she writes. For the impatient critic to perceive, understand and appreciate such *flowings-into* a life, "influences," is far harder than to catalogue quotations, paraphrases and echoes.

In "The Artist," Levertov celebrates the true artist who, willingly exposed to all the turmoil of life, "maintains dialogue with his heart, meets things with his mind." Her vocation was to be "the poet in the world," living out her social, political, and spiritual convictions and bringing them into her writing. The Vietnam War drove her into intense political organizing, draft resistance demonstrations, arrests, and illegal travel to North Vietnam. Her sister's death, the war and the social unrest associated with it, kindled in her an apocalyptic anger, grief and despair which lasted the rest of her life and suffused much of her writing. The most negative criticism of her political poetry mourned that her engagement made her poetry "strident," and argued that she had lost much of the exploratory, energetic quality of her earlier work. Disagreement over her political poetry estranged Levertov and Robert Duncan for most of the rest of his life.

Albert Gelpi tells us that in the poetry of her early maturity, *The Jacob's Ladder* (1961) and *O Taste and See* (1964) "the poems again and again break into a celebration of the sacredness, even the sacramentality of temporal experience...."[4] In her own writing about poetry, as well as the critics' assessment, reference to the sacred, the sacramental and incantational frequently appear. Apocalypse shakes all foundations. Levertov's affirmative spirituality, "arrogant in innocence," darkened into doubt. Images of wandering and pilgrimage, always common in her poetry, take on greater resonance. At times all she can hold onto is a determination not to give up life, even when the place of pilgrimage is without meaning; "this is not the place,/The spirit's left it." She asks herself whether twenty years of poetry has been merely deathsongs:

Is there anything
I write any more that is not
elegy?

Levertov's pilgrimage ultimately leads her over her later years
"from a regretful skepticism which sought relief in some
measure of pantheism (while it acknowledges both the ethical
and emotional influence of my Jewish-Christian roots and
early education) to a position of Christian belief."[5] Because
she is a poet, she writes, she has faith in what Keats called *the
truth of the imagination,* and following the road of imagina-
tion "I've come to see certain analogies, and also some inter-
action, between the journey of art and the journey of faith."[6]
To begin a work of art, she believes, "resembles moving from
intellectual assent to opening the acts of daily life to perme-
ation by religious faith." The *interaction* between the journeys
of art and faith brought her to poems (exploring what she calls
"do-it-yourself theology"), the first of which was a piece dedi-
cated to Doubting Thomas, "Mass for the Day of St. Thomas
Didymus." The poem began as an experiment in structure:

> an agnostic Mass ..., basing each part on what seemed its pri-
> mal character: the Kyrie a cry for mercy, the Gloria a praise-
> song, the Credo an individual assertion, and so on: each a per-
> sonal, secular meditation. But a few months later, when I
> arrived at the Agnus Dei, I discovered myself to be in a differ-
> ent relationship to the material and to the liturgical form from
> that in which I had begun. The experience of writing the
> poem—that long swim through waters of unknown depth—
> had also been a conversion process....[7]

From the book *Candles in Babylon* (1982) through her final
six collections of poetry, Levertov continued to explore, with
greater intensity and clarity, both the interactions of those two
journeys of art and faith, as well as the *place* of double vision,
the borderland, where she typically locates the artist, the pil-
grim, the wanderer, the mystic and the saint. Though still pro-
foundly engaged by her political and social concerns, her
poetry, she says in "Some Affinities of Content" (1991), also

sought to pursue a spiritual quest which opened her to poems of the wilderness-world centered on Buddhist or Native American belief systems and poems rooted in a Christian or Jewish context, which explored the struggle between faith and doubt, epiphanies, "explorations and illuminations of Biblical scenes or sayings."[8] Long influenced by such writers and activists as Dorothy Day, Thomas Merton and the Berrigans, Levertov also found loving friends in Seattle in a worship-community of Catholic social-activists and became a Roman Catholic.

Just as some critics found her political themes hard to accept, some have found her religious themes uncongenial. Religious poetry and political have this in common: where the writer speaks out of personal experience and deep feelings, the reader who shares neither may perceive only abstractions and tendentious opinions. The writer tries to speak of the flesh-and-blood experience which informs beliefs and convictions; readers who have not shared the same or similar experience may see only poeticized doctrine—unfamiliar to some, too familiar to others, a source of resentment to still others. To carry the reluctant or resistant reader along on the double journey of art and faith, this *poetic faith,* everything depends on how well the poet can ground the sensation and feelings, the testing of faith and doubt, belief and disbelief in the poetry and invite the reader to participate with the poet in a process of exploration and discovery. It is fitting that Levertov's patron saint should be Doubting Thomas, that her poems should be, in the title of her 1984 volume, *Oblique Prayers,* and that her posthumous volume (1999) should commemorate *This Great Unknowing.*

* * *

In this selection of poems we have tried to give fair representation to each part of Levertov's career and to her dominant themes and concerns. Thus there are poems about her parents and sister, her marriage and her relations with her husband and son; a fair sampling of love poems; political and religious and ecologically-focused poems; poems growing out of her dream-life; poems celebrating poetic influences on her life; lyrics, meditations, narratives and elegies. We have also tried to give a fair balance to what might be thought of as the three large periods of her literary life: First, from her first works through *O Taste and See*—the period when she was praised by the greatest number of critics for her "sacramental" and celebratory vision, and when she is most obviously influenced by Williams and learning American speech; Second, the period from *The Sorrow Dance* through *Life in the Forest,* when she is most overtly, but never exclusively, political in her writing, most torn by doubts about her poetic vision, given over to grief at loss of her sister and her mother, and when her marriage ends; Third, the period from *Candles in Babylon* to *This Great Unknowing,* when she has returned to her Christian roots, then extended into Catholicism, and when she has moved to Seattle and is engaged by the sensibilities and themes of some of the writers of the Northwest.

PAUL A. LACEY

1. *Bloodaxe Anthology of Women Poets,* 1985.

2. Sutton, Walter, "A Conversation with Denise Levertov," in *Conversations with Denise Levertov,* Jewel Spears Brooker, ed., University Press of Mississippi: 1998, 23.

3. Sutton, 23.

4. Gelpi, Albert, ed., *Denise Levertov: Selected Criticism,* University of Michigan Press: 1991, 4.

5. Levertov, Denise, *New and Selected Essays,* New Directions: 1992, 242–43.

6. *NSE* 248–49.

7. *NSE* 250.

8. *NSE* 5–6.

61   'Olga Poems.' The quoted lines in the sixth section are an adapta-
     tion of some lines in 'Selva Oscura' by the late Louis MacNeice, a
     poem much loved by my sister.

95   'Gandhi's Gun (and Brecht's Vow).' *'Keiner/oder Alle, Alles/oder
     Nichts!'* The lines from Brecht are a refrain of a song about slaves
     casting off their chains: 'No one or everyone, all or nothing!'

99   'The Old King.' The italicized lines are from Edmund Waller
     (1606–87).

100 'Memories of John Keats.' The italicized words are all from John
     Keats's letters, as in the phrase 'the Vale of Soulmaking.' The 'Vale
     of Health' is a part of Hampstead Heath, London, near which the
     poet lived.

112 'Chekhov on the West Heath.' The West Heath is a section of
     Hampstead Heath, the tract of never-cultivated land that over-
     looks London from the north and includes the point of highest el-
     evation in the London area.

113 'The small, dark-green volumes. / The awkward, heroic versions'
     refers to the English collected edition of Constance Garnett's pio-
     neer translations.

     Für Elise is a short piano piece by Beethoven.

114 'The Black Monk' is a Chekhov story often, or perhaps I should say
     usually, interpreted quite differently–that is, as being a sad story
     about illusion. I did not then, and do not now, see it that way. All
     the *apparent* illusion in it is in fact what is strong and positive!

     'The betrothed girl' is the heroine of the story variously translated
     as 'The Betrothed,' 'A Marriageable Girl,' 'The Bride,' etc.

116 'tender, delightful, ironic'–from Gorki's reminiscences of Che-
     khov. However, just about everyone who ever described Chekhov
     mentioned his smile in very similar terms.

125 'The Dragon-Fly Mother.' Readers may be interested to read 'The
     Earthwoman and the Waterwoman' (*Collected Earlier Poems,*
     p. 31), a poem written in 1957, to which this 1979 poem makes
     some allusions.

137 'Beginners.' The opening stanza is Swinburne, slightly misquoted because I had remembered it this way for many years.

146 'The Servant Girl at Emmaus.' The painting is in the collection a Russborough House, County Wicklow, Ireland. Before it was cleaned, the subject was not apparent; only when the figures at table in a room behind her were revealed was her previously ambiguous expression clearly legible as acutely attentive.

149 'Caedmon.' The story comes, of course, from The Venerable Bede's *History of the English Church and People*, but I first read it as a child in John Richard Green's *History of the English People*, 1855. The poem forms a companion piece to 'St. Peter and the Angel' in *Oblique Prayers*.

150 'Making Peace.' 'The imagination of disaster' is Henry James's phrase. He said Americans had it—but do they still? Imagination is what makes reality real to the mind (which is why it's so hard to imagine peace, for it has not been experienced in the reality of our life in history except as the absence of war). Yet not only peace but the disastrous realities of our time go unimagined, even when 'known about,' when 'psychic numbing' veils them; and thus the energy to act constructively, which *imaginative* knowledge could generate, is repressed.

152 'On a Theme from Julian's Chapter XX.' This is from the longer text of Julian of Norwich's *Showings* (or *Revelations*). The quoted lines follow the Grace Warrack transcription (1901). Warrack uses the word 'kinship' in her title-heading for the chapter, though in the text itself she says 'kindness,' thus—as in her Glossary—reminding one of the roots common to both words.

154 'The Showings.' The quotations are taken from the *Pelican* and the *Classics of Western Spirituality* editions.

161 'Variations on Themes by Rilke.' Those who read German will be able to see what images and ideas are taken from the original and which are my own.

172 'To Rilke.' The allusion is to Rilke's prose piece 'Concerning the Poet' (*Where Silence Reigns,* New Directions).

188 'Conversion of Brother Lawrence.' The quotations are from Brother Lawrence's 'The Practice of the Presence of God,' available in many editions), and the biographical allusions are based on the original introduction.

INDEX OF TITLES AND FIRST LINES

218

New Directions Paperbooks—a partial listing

Siegfried Lenz, The German Lesson
Alexander Lernet-Holenia, Count Luna
Denise Levertov, Selected Poems
Li Po, Selected Poems
Clarice Lispector, The Hour of the Star
  The Passion According to G. H.
Federico García Lorca, Selected Poems*
Nathaniel Mackey, Splay Anthem
Xavier de Maistre, Voyage Around My Room
Stéphane Mallarmé, Selected Poetry and Prose*
Javier Marías, Your Face Tomorrow (3 volumes)
Adam Mars-Jones, Box Hill
Bernadette Mayer, Midwinter Day
Carson McCullers, The Member of the Wedding
Fernando Melchor, Hurricane Season
Thomas Merton, New Seeds of Contemplation
  The Way of Chuang Tzu
Henri Michaux, A Barbarian in Asia
Dunya Mikhail, The Beekeeper
Henry Miller, The Colossus of Maroussi
  Big Sur & the Oranges of Hieronymus Bosch
Yukio Mishima, Confessions of a Mask
  Death in Midsummer
Eugenio Montale, Selected Poems*
Vladimir Nabokov, Laughter in the Dark
  Nikolai Gogol
Pablo Neruda, The Captain's Verses*
  Love Poems*
Charles Olson, Selected Writings
George Oppen, New Collected Poems
Wilfred Owen, Collected Poems
Hiroko Oyamada, The Hole
José Emilio Pacheco, Battles in the Desert
Michael Palmer, Little Elegies for Sister Satan
Nicanor Parra, Antipoems*
Boris Pasternak, Safe Conduct
Octavio Paz, Poems of Octavio Paz
Victor Pelevin, Omon Ra
Georges Perec, Ellis Island
Alejandra Pizarnik
  Extracting the Stone of Madness
Ezra Pound, The Cantos
  New Selected Poems and Translations
Raymond Queneau, Exercises in Style
Qian Zhongshu, Fortress Besieged
Herbert Read, The Green Child
Kenneth Rexroth, Selected Poems
Keith Ridgway, A Shock

Rainer Maria Rilke
  Poems from the Book of Hours
Arthur Rimbaud, Illuminations*
  A Season in Hell and The Drunken Boat*
Evelio Rosero, The Armies
Fran Ross, Oreo
Joseph Roth, The Emperor's Tomb
Raymond Roussel, Locus Solus
Ihara Saikaku, The Life of an Amorous Woman
Nathalie Sarraute, Tropisms
Jean-Paul Sartre, Nausea
Judith Schalansky, An Inventory of Losses
Delmore Schwartz
  In Dreams Begin Responsibilities
W. G. Sebald, The Emigrants
  The Rings of Saturn
Anne Serre, The Governesses
Patti Smith, Woolgathering
Stevie Smith, Best Poems
  Novel on Yellow Paper
Gary Snyder, Turtle Island
Dag Solstad, Professor Andersen's Night
Muriel Spark, The Driver's Seat
Maria Stepanova, In Memory of Memory
Wislawa Szymborska, How to Start Writing
Antonio Tabucchi, Pereira Maintains
Junichiro Tanizaki, The Maids
Yoko Tawada, The Emissary
  Memoirs of a Polar Bear
Dylan Thomas, A Child's Christmas in Wales
  Collected Poems
Tomas Tranströmer, The Great Enigma
Leonid Tsypkin, Summer in Baden-Baden
Tu Fu, Selected Poems
Paul Valéry, Selected Writings
Enrique Vila-Matas, Bartleby & Co.
Elio Vittorini, Conversations in Sicily
Rosmarie Waldrop, The Nick of Time
Robert Walser, The Assistant
  The Tanners
Eliot Weinberger, An Elemental Thing
  The Ghosts of Birds
Nathanael West, The Day of the Locust
  Miss Lonelyhearts
Tennessee Williams, The Glass Menagerie
  A Streetcar Named Desire
William Carlos Williams, Selected Poems
Louis Zukofsky, "A"

*BILINGUAL EDITION

For a complete listing, request a free catalog from New Directions, 80 8th Avenue, New York, NY 10011
or visit us online at **ndbooks.com**